VEIN OF

LIFE

VEIN OF
LIFE

by Mary Muller

THE BOBBS-MERRILL COMPANY, INC.
A Subsidiary of Howard W. Sams & Co., Inc., Publishers
INDIANAPOLIS · KANSAS CITY · NEW YORK

Author's note: This is a true story. All the characters in this book are living, and all the letters are authentic. The names of the doctors have been changed.

This book
is dedicated to Nicky's grandmother
Mary Pauline Muller

CONTENTS

THE
CRUCIAL
YEARS

Part I

CHAPTER 1

THIS is the story of our son Nicolas. He was not our only child. Bill and I married in 1938 when the lowering clouds of war were gathering in Europe. A year later, when the storm broke, our daughter Dorothy was born. We called her Dot. She was fair-haired, brown-eyed and very shy.

Two years later, our second daughter, Susan, was born. We called her Sue. Dark-haired, brown-eyed. She was warm, affectionate, and placid. This placidity, I found to my regret, was to be short lived.

We built our house on the crest of Wynberg Hill, beneath the massive and protective shoulder of Table Mountain. A great granite boulder stood behind the house and outcrops of grey rock were scattered over the property, so we called it Greystones. A garden began to develop around the house, and each year it extended a little farther. Here in this cool and

3

deeply acid soil, rhododendrons, azaleas and camellias flourished, and the hydrangeas were dark blue.

We overlooked the sweep of Constantia Valley and faced across to the Muizenberg Mountains and the waters of False Bay. The view of the valley became part of our lives and with each season it changed. In the winter the northwest wind swept down the valley, uprooting trees and leaving devastation in its wake, to be followed by the heavy winter rains. The crenelated crags of Constantiaberg would be hidden under swollen black-grey clouds, her flanks furred with green pines. In the hollow, the leafless oaks were misty grey. The newly dug furrows between the vines formed a sharply etched herringbone. The sea, bleak and cold, merged into the grey horizon.

In the summer the herringboned vineyards were green, the oaks lush and cool looking, and the sea shimmering bright blue. Behind us, Table Mountain was covered with a table-cloth of white, smooth cloud.

The war was over. The business was doing well. We were comfortably off, and the children were strong and healthy. These were the good years.

When Dot and Sue were babies, I was charmed by Bill's tenderness and love for them. Each morning he rose early and brought them to our room, pink and glowing, diapers changed. In the evenings he sat and played with them for hours.

As they grew older, I made the discovery that he was a doting and indulgent father. They adored him, ignored him, and took the fullest advantage of his good nature.

It fell to me to chastise them and correct them.

Dirk was born when Sue was ten. He was born by caesarean section, entering the world seven weeks too soon. He weighed three and a half pounds; his legs were as thick as my little finger and he had the tiny wizened face of an old man. From the moment he made his appearance into the world, bawling lustily, he seized hold of life with minute, clawlike hands, and hung on grimly.

Years later the pediatrician who cared for him after his birth said to me: "Dirk is the toughest premature baby I have ever handled; and I've handled hundreds." His hair was fair, and he was to be our only blue-eyed child.

Nicolas was born four years later. He had fair hair and hazel eyes. We called him Nicky.

A few days after he was born, the same shaggy-haired pediatrician who had looked after Dirk came in to see me.

"Your son is coming along. Funny thing, you know, he has a blue tongue like a chow. Sometimes the babies absorb the blue dye from the name tape around their wrists. I tested him for this, but it was negative."

The next day I got a thrombosis in my leg, and the following week, my father died.

The bad years had begun.

My leg kept me confined in bed for several weeks. Nicky was well cared for by Sister Stewart, who had looked after Dirk with efficiency and gentleness after he was born.

When Nicky was five weeks old and I was once again on my feet, starting to hobble around the house with painful slowness, our shaggy-haired pediatrician telephoned me.

"I'm coming along this morning to give Nicky a final check-up, and then I'll say cheerio. Dr. Jones is meeting me at your home: she will be bringing her electro-cardiogram along."

When they arrived, I escorted them to Nicky's room and stood watching for a few moments.

I was expecting two friends for tea, so I left them and went to the kitchen to tell the cook to bake scones.

I looked out of the window to see Dirk happily engaged making a castle in the white sand beneath the loquat tree.

Half an hour later Sister Stewart called me.

"The doctor is leaving. He would like to see you before he goes."

He was standing in the sitting room with his back to the light.

"Well, how is he?" I asked, smiling.

"Not altogether satisfactory. His heart is not a hundred percent."

"His heart!"

"Yes. I have never been altogether happy about him. His blueness has been a problem and his development has not been satisfactory. He is what is known as a 'blue baby.' "

My own heart had almost stopped.

"What does that mean?"

"It means that he has been born with a congenital heart defect."

"How bad is it? Can anything be done for him?"

"At this stage it is impossible to tell what heart defect he has. He is only five weeks old. When he is 18 months you must take him to a physician. He will have X rays taken and will be able to tell you more than I can at this moment. Fantastic strides have been made in cardiac surgery during the last ten years and you are fortunate Nicky is your youngest child. Ten years ago nothing could have been done for him."

We shook hands, and I said good-by.

Sister Stewart was standing silently beside me during our conversation.

"He didn't want to tell you, but I told him you are the kind who would want to know immediately."

I nodded. "You're right."

"I've been so desperately worried about Nicky. I've known for some time there has been something wrong with him. Sometimes it took him three hours to finish his bottle. Even his flesh felt wrong to me."

I left her and walked into the hall, unplugging the telephone. I slowly hobbled up the stairs to our bedroom. I picked up the phone.

"Will you put me through to Mr. Muller, please."

6

Bill's voice came through, strong and cheerful.

"Hello."

"Darling. The doctor has just told me that there is something wrong with Nicky's heart."

There was dead silence.

Then he said abruptly, "I'll be home in 20 minutes."

I replaced the receiver and walked slowly into Nicky's room.

He was asleep. He did not then have the purplish blueness we were to see later. His flesh was white, faintly tinged with blue, like watered-down milk.

I looked at him.

Oh God. What is your future? What suffering is in store for you? What is going to happen to you?

I returned to my room, closed the door, and sank onto my bed, at last giving way to the tears which were choking me. I sobbed in abandoned grief.

There was a knock on the door.

"Mrs. Muller," said Sister Stewart, "your friends have arrived." I sat up and tried to steady my voice.

"Tell them I can't see them. Tell them what has happened. They will understand."

I rose and ran some cold water into the basin and bathed my face.

Ten minutes later Bill walked into our room. He was pale and his face was drawn. He walked across the room, put his arm around my shoulder and kissed me. Life was never the same for us after this.

CHAPTER 2

The other children felt our anxiety; something light as gossamer had vanished. It was not happiness—it was perhaps that neither of us felt completely carefree and light-hearted again.

During the next years Nicky's development was slow. He did not thrive, nor did he slip back. He caught a cold, which caused us deep alarm; his labored breathing was frightening. He was ashen and his lips were blue. With painful slowness he won this battle, like some tiny craft weathering a dark storm.

Dot and Sue helped me look after him. They were seventeen and fifteen respectively. They fed him, bathed him, and played with him. He was always conscious of being surrounded by love, and he responded to this with happy affection. It was soon evident that he was mentally alert and highly intelligent.

His appetite was birdlike, but he slowly put on weight. When he was a year old he started to crawl, awkwardly and sluggishly. A heave forward, a rest, lying on his stomach. Another heave; another rest.

When Nicky was two he took his first steps, and by the time he was two and one-half he could walk. He could only manage very short distances, and then he squatted on his haunches; this strange hunched posture seemed to enable him to fill his lungs. Whenever he was tired, he sat crouched in this position, his face blue and intense.

The time had arrived for us to have him examined by a physician. Bill telephoned and made the appointment. The following week we drove in to Cape Town, down the rubber tree avenue, past the famous Kirstenbosch Botanical Gardens. We drove between the tall oaks of Newlands Avenue, like the cool, green interior of a gothic church. We drove past the Zoo, and the compact buildings of the University of Cape Town: the only buildings on the mountain side of the road, until we reached the outskirts of the city. These slopes of Devil's Peak and Table Mountain given to the nation by Cecil Rhodes to be preserved for all time in their natural beauty; camps of green grass stretching up the slopes of Devil's Peak, edged with cluster-pines and the umbrella shaped stone-pines; where zebra, fallow deer, wildebeest, springbok and eland graze in peace. We could see the Medical Centre amongst the new skyscrapers on the Foreshore; it was built on ground reclaimed from the sea. The cars in the carpark glittered like tinsel in the bright sun.

Nicky sat on my lap, happy and excited. Bill and I were strained and silent.

Dr. Thomas was a big friendly man who handled Nicky with gentle competence. When he had completed his examination, he called in a nurse to do an electro-cardiograph. Nicky endured these indignities with submissive bewilderment.

We were sent upstairs to have X-ray photographs taken.

"I'd like to see you both here next Monday at 10:30 A.M. with Nicky. I will then have had an opportunity to study the

X rays and cardiograph and will be in a position to give you an opinion on his condition."

For the rest of that week we tried to put it out of our minds, but were able to think of little else.

When we met him again, he greeted us with a friendly smile, picking up Nicky and placing him on his knee.

"I've been studying the X rays and cardiograph and would diagnose your son as having Fallots Tetralogy. This means there is a severe narrowing at the origin of the pulmonary artery and a large hole between the wall of the two ventricles. When the right ventricle contracts, its blue blood is ejected more readily through the hole in the left ventricle and aorta than into the pulmonary artery. This shunting of blue blood into the left side of the heart where the blood is normally bright red, having been oxygenated by the lungs, results in cyanosis or blueness of the body, characteristic of the 'blue baby.' You will find that during exercise the blueness will become more pronounced, resulting in shortness of breath and tiredness. Of course, a catheterization will have to be done before any diagnosis will be acceptable."

He smiled.

"I am sorry. I was hoping that he would only have a hole in the heart. Today, that is almost looked upon as a minor operation. However, they have been operating on Fallots Tetralogy at the Mayo Clinic with great success for the last ten years and I would advise you to take him there when the time comes."

He drew a diagram and explained to us what was wrong with Nicky's heart, and how it could be repaired.

"Does he squat when he is tired?"

"Yes."

"That is typical. You will also find that as he gets older the tips of his fingers will become clubbed."

He picked up Nicky's fingers and looked at them.

"You can already see that they are thickening. A year after

the operation the clubbing will disappear and he will have normal hands."

"Would this operation enable him to lead a normal life?"

"Definitely. It would certainly give him a 95 percent heart, which is better than most of us." He smiled.

"At the moment nothing can be done for him—he is still too young. The ideal operative age is six."

"How much may we allow him to do now? May he walk about as much as he wants to?"

"Don't you worry about that. He'll decide himself how much he can do. There's no danger that he will overtire himself.

"When the time comes, I'll be able to make the necessary arrangements for you. They are doing wonders at the Mayo Clinic and have some of the most famous heart surgeons in the world there."

On the way home, holding Nicky tightly in my arms, I said to Bill: "I feel so much happier now. In spite of all the anxiety we will have to face over the operation, we now know he has a future and he will be able to lead a normal life."

Bill was silent. I knew that he was thinking of the suffering in store for his little son whom he loved so dearly.

CHAPTER 3

Six months later, Bill flew to Europe on a short business trip. With him, he took the full set of Nicky's X-ray photographs. He had written and made an appointment with the most eminent heart physician in London. He had also made a further appointment with a leading heart surgeon in Dusseldorf. We were exploring every channel.

Ten days later he wrote to me.

"The day before my appointment with Dr. Macdonald, I telephoned him and he said he would see me at the hospital. I will never forget my visit there. It is situated in a rather dirty and dingy part of London and from the outside looks more like an old-fashioned prison than a hospital. The place was obviously very ancient and the entrance barred by large iron gates. I wondered, as I walked through the courtyards and corridors, if Nicky's operation would take place here. It appears a very depressing place.

"I found Dr. Macdonald an elderly man with grey hair, a bright complexion, and very bushy eyebrows. There was no mistaking his origin. His accent was broad Scots.

"He asked me many questions about Nicky and I did my best to give him a complete picture. He then studied the X rays for some time and I was dismayed to notice the expression about his mouth become grim. He said: 'I am not prepared to give any definite opinion on your son. The fact that I have not seen him makes it very difficult, but my study of the X-ray photographs leads me to think that the circulation of blood in the lung is very reduced, and at this stage I would not recommend surgery. Your son is very young, however, and heart surgery is developing so fast that you should not lose hope.'

"He says that heart surgery in the United States has far outstripped all other countries, though doctors in Britain hope to catch up one day.

"I feel far from happy. I can only say that my visit to Dr. Macdonald has been a disappointment."

Two weeks later a letter arrived from Germany.

"My appointment with Dr. Schumann was for 11 A.M. and I arrived on time at the huge Clinic which has just been built for him.

"How different this was from the hospital in London. Several modern buildings, each one six stories high, and inside, everything clean, polished, and new.

"After waiting for an hour, I was ushered into Dr. Schumann's room. He immediately stood up and extended a huge hand. He was very warm and friendly and said: 'So you come all the way from Cape Town in South Africa to see me about your boy. Well, tell me all about him and show me photographs and X-ray photographs.'

"I went through it all again, as I had done with Dr. Macdonald. He then studied the X rays at great length and, to my amazement, suddenly commenced banging on the desk with his large fist, shouting '*Nicht operieren! Nicht operieren! Nicht operieren!'* When he had calmed down he said: 'You must on no account allow your son to be operated on. The time will come when surgery has advanced to such an extent that an operation may be successful, but you should wait as long as possible, up to another eight years or even ten years.' "

The channels we had explored had proved fruitless and disquieting. On Bill they had a depressive effect. Now, when I spoke of Nicky's operation and future, he remained silent and brooding.

Nicky continued to progress slowly. He spent most of the morning playing in the garden or around the house. He was unable to venture far into the garden. In the afternoon he slept deeply, for many hours. Most of the time he was sweet-tempered and adult for his age, and it was easy to reason with him. He was, however, becoming dimly aware that he was the focal point at Greystones. He was beginning to sense our over-protective love and our barely concealed anxiety.

He worshipped Bill, and tyrannized him. No sooner did his father come home in the evening than he became whining and demanding; screaming with temper if he was thwarted.

On the occasions when he was naughty and had a tantrum, I spanked him, as I spanked all my children when they deserved it. When this happened, he sulked and glowered at me, turning his face away if I tried to kiss him. Nevertheless, it had the effect of making him tractable and amiable.

Bill on rare occasions took his hand back and delivered a well deserved swipe on the bottom. Dot always said: "I'd rather have ten of your smacks, Mom, than one of those awful hard ones of Dad's."

He could not bring himself to smack Nicky, however much he deserved it. Even when his small son pummeled him in a fit of screaming temper, he sat quietly, looking at him reproachfully, an expression of deep sadness on his face.

I invited other children to play with him. It was not successful. He was an uncooperative and demanding host and they soon became bored with him and the restrictions of the house; they ran outside and followed Dirk, who did nothing to discourage their attentions. Unable to follow them, Nicky remained in the nursery crying piteously.

The realization was slowly dawning on him that he was different from other children.

Dot was now at the art school. She was 19, fair and petite, and still incurably shy. She had the gift of quiet companionship, and we were very close. She was like a second mother to Nicky and always called him Nod.

Sue was going through all the uncertainty and insecurity of adolescence. Warmhearted and affectionate, she more than anyone could make Nicky burst into delighted chuckles of laughter. She was easily upset and quickly bored—I found her exhausting and exasperating.

Dirk was now at the preparatory school. He was passionately eager to be an athlete and excel at games. We gave him a brindled boxer and named her Sarah. The two of them disappeared for hours, combing the forest and exploring the streams in the valley below us. Often he came back with a basket of mushrooms, a fern, or a wilted plant he had dug up for my garden. Often he teased Nicky in a pathetic attempt to draw attention to himself.

Just as my children had grown and developed in the last few years, so, too, a change had taken place in Cape Town which interested us deeply. We now had a Cardiac Clinic with world recognition, and a heart surgeon who was performing open-heart surgery with brilliant success.

CHAPTER 4

ONE summer's day in 1937, when Bill and I were planning to get married, he stopped his car on the top of Wynberg Hill and we fought our way through the dense undergrowth and blackberries to scale the thirty-foot-high beacon-topped granite boulder which now stands behind our home. We were on the border of the Hohenort Estate, which belonged to old Arnold Wilhelm Spilhaus, Bill's grandfather. For the first time I saw the panoramic view of the Constantia Valley and False Bay: the indigo blue sea; the Muizenberg Mountains palely grey in the summer haze; the green vines; the oak forest through which we could see the stepped gables and red roof of Hohenort.

"What do you think of the view?" Bill asked.

"Fantastic!" I said, ruefully looking at the hole in my stocking.

"How would you like to live here?"

"Live here! What do you mean?"

"Grandfather offered this piece of ground to my parents but they aren't interested in building here. Perhaps I may be able to persuade him to sell it to us."

I looked at the ground immediately below us. It was thickly wooded, the indigenous trees fighting a losing battle against the imported wattle and pine. Fifty years ago the southern slopes of Wynberg Hill had gleamed with the lustrous sheen of thousands of silver trees; temperamental and shortlived, unable to fight for their existence against the exotic invaders, now few were left. I saw a gnarled wild laurel, growing against a cluster of granite rocks.

"We must save that," I said. "I think we should build our house to the right, so we'll be able to see that wonderful old tree from our sitting room window."

Grandfather sold us two acres of ground for five hundred and seventy-five dollars.

"I can't give it to you. My heirs might object."

His eyes twinkled and his fine old bearded face was wreathed in smiles.

However, Bill's mother gave it to us for a wedding present. This was the first of many generous gifts we were to receive from her during our lives.

In 1907 Grandfather Spilhaus bought one half of the Klaassenbosch farm, in the Constantia Valley. This included the beautiful old thatched homestead, which unfortunately did not conform to his ideas of comfort; he demolished it and on the site built a great house, with the stepped gables so typical of the business houses in his home town, Lubeck. He named his new estate Hohenort, which means "The High Place."

Often on Sunday, up to twenty of us sat down to lunch. My mother-in-law deftly carved the chickens or the great sirloins of beef. The old people sat at the round table at the end of the dining room, and the rest of us at the long table which ran the length of the room. In the summer great bowls of red and white hanepoot grapes stood on the sideboard. It was a big, warm house, always filled with people. After Grandfather's death, Hohenort was sold; the beautiful farm was broken up, and the big house became a private hotel.

My own family played a smaller role in our children's lives. My mother, who was my closest friend, died before we were married, and they never saw my father frequently enough to become close to him.

Nicky was lonely. Sue had joined Dot at the art school, and Dirk was at school all morning.

I discussed it with my mother-in-law. She has always played a big part in our lives. Her gaiety and cheerfulness endeared her to all our children.

"Do you think it would be a good idea to send Nicky to a nursery school? He's so lonely now the other children are away all day."

"I think it's a very good idea. All the children went to nursery school when they were his age."

"I know, but Nicky isn't good with strange children. He won't be able to join in their games. I'm so afraid he will be unhappy, and they will be unkind to him."

"My dear, the only way for Nicky to learn to get on with other children is to mix with them. He'll have to go to school sooner or later. I'm sure once he's there he'll enjoy it and be happy."

I knew we could not protect him much longer.

I was deeply worried when I took him to school that first day, remembering how bitterly Dirk had cried four years ago when I left him there. Whatever Nicky may have felt, he remained inscrutable and shed no tears when I departed.

Four hours later, on fetching him, he greeted me unsmilingly. On the way to the car he said with disgust:

"I don't like going to school with girls."

He climbed into the car, and as the engine started, added bitterly:

"Dirk hasn't got to go to school with girls."

He enjoyed his work at school, and it was soon evident he could hold his own in class with his companions. Nevertheless, as I had feared, he was not happy. Now, for the first time, he got the full impact of his difference from other children. He could not play on the swings or run around the garden with them at playtime. He withdrew from them, and in the organized class games in which he could participate, he became uncooperative and unresponsive. I am sure he often felt tired and unwell.

He made no friends and waited with consuming impatience to join Dirk at the preparatory school, convinced that there everything would be different.

He was nearing his operative age, and the time had come for us to seek a second opinion.

I telephoned and made an appointment with Dr. de Goede, a leading physician in Cape Town.

At five, Nicky was small for his age. During the last few years he had become perceptibly bluer. His color varied greatly according to the weather; intense heat or cold brought a purplish tinge to his cheeks and a blueness to his lips. On the day that we had our appointment, the weather was mild and his color was almost normal. When we walked into the room, Dr. de Goede stood up and shook hands with both of us. I sat down in the seat opposite the desk and studied him closely. I liked what I saw: there was sensitivity, humor and warmth.

We spoke of trivialities for a few moments, then he smiled and said:

"Why have you brought your son to see me?"

"He has got Fallots Tetralogy."

The smile remained. He said quietly:

"I may not agree with that diagnosis."

"This is why I have brought him to you. My husband and I feel that we should have a second opinion."

He took Nicky's hands and looked at them. The clubbed fingertips were now noticeable.

"Well, Nicky." He smiled. "Let me have a look at you."

I helped Nicky undress. Without his clothes he looked pathetic, his body thin and his legs undeveloped and knock-kneed.

While he was being examined he never took his eyes off me. He submitted to the electro-cardiogram, his eyes fixed on mine with an inscrutable expression. After he was X-rayed, I dressed him and sat down facing Dr. de Goede.

"I am not entirely satisfied with the present diagnosis. With Fallots Tetralogy there should be a pronounced heart murmur. In Nicky's case I cannot hear anything. I would like you to bring him to the Cardiac Clinic next Wednesday and we'll have his heartbeat projected onto a sensitive phono-cardiograph; this amplifies the heartbeat. Maybe I shall be able to hear it then."

He paused.

"I think the time is now right for Nicky to have a cardiac catheterization done."

"What is that?"

"It's an exploratory examination which will assist us to arrive at a correct diagnosis. He will have to go to hospital for two days. A thin plastic tube will be pushed up a vein in his arm into the heart cavity and will explore the different chambers. Pressure can be recorded and oxygen content measured electronically. We inject radio-opaque dye through the tube and take X-ray photographs which should enable us to find out what defects he has."

"Will he be unconscious when all this is done?"

"No, he has to cooperate and help us."

Seeing my horrified expression, he said:

"He won't feel pain. He'll be uncomfortable. A catheterization must be done before cardiac surgery can take place. No surgeon will attempt to operate unless he knows what he has to repair. The catheterizations done in our Clinic are accepted at the Mayo Clinic without question."

He paused.

"As you know, we have a brilliant heart surgeon in Cape Town, with world recognition, and a highly experienced team handling the heart and lung machine."

"Yes, I know. We've been reading about the successful heart operations in the newspapers, and it's given us great hope."

"They have performed operations on Fallots Tetralogy in Cape Town many times with complete success. It will no longer be necessary for you to take him to the Mayo Clinic."

"That would make all the difference," I said. "I'm sure it would help him to have the family near him at that time. When do you think the catheterization should be done?"

"As soon as possible. I'll make the arrangements and let you know."

He smiled.

"I'll see you then on Wednesday at three o' clock at Groote Schuur Hospital. Come in at the side entrance, and I'll meet you there."

We met him there, on Wednesday, at the time arranged.

Nicky lay on a couch, his eyes wide, as he listened to his own heartbeat sounding like a drum.

Dr. de Goede walked down to our car with us. As he opened the door I said:

"Could you hear anything on the amplifier?"

He smiled gently.

"No. I'm sorry. I could hear nothing."

CHAPTER 5

THE catheterization took place ten days later. Dr. de Goede's secretary telephoned me. "The Doctor would like you to take Nicky to Groote Schuur Hospital at two o' clock on Wednesday afternoon, the day before the catheterization. You will receive a card for Nicky in the mail, and this must be handed in at the office when you arrive. You may visit him on Thursday afternoon, and Dr. de Goede will see you at the hospital at ten o' clock on Friday morning."

Nicky thought he was about to set out upon a great adventure. In his small mind he pictured something new and exciting, with himself the central figure. The morning we drove to the hospital, his face was glowing and his eyes were bright. On the velvety sward below the Rhodes Memorial, two fallow deer, grazing near the fence, lifted their heads and looked at us as we drove past. On the corner, where we turned off to the hospital, the green verge swept up towards the crags of Devil's

Peak, and a herd of zebra were superimposed against the dark background of the stone pines. The red roofs and the white walls of the big hospital were before us. He craned his neck out of the window.

"Gee, Mom, it's big!"

We walked through the door and found the entrance hall packed with humanity. There was no place where Nicky could sit so I placed his suitcase against the wall.

"Sit on this, darling. I will be back in a few minutes."

I waited at the office window. A man at the desk looked up, then continued with his work. He rose and walked out of the room. Gone for five minutes, he came back and sat down once more at the desk. Ultimately, he reluctantly dragged himself to his feet, greeted me without a smile, and held out his hand for the envelope I was holding. He asked me questions and filled in a form.

I looked at his cold face, his humorless mouth without pity or warmth. I thought of all the people who came to this window; people who were frightened, people who were to suffer, people who needed kindness and reassurance. How many of them must have been chilled by this reception.

When I rejoined Nicky, I could see that the cold edge had already touched his spirit. The brightness had left his eyes and his grip tightened on my hand.

We took the elevator to the third floor and walked down the corridor to the children's ward. The nurse in charge greeted us with a kindly smile that did much to dispel my depression.

The children's ward was full. We were taken to the only empty bed, and a young nurse quickly undressed Nicky and put him to bed.

His lips were trembling; his eyes swept the ward with incredulous dismay. A baby in a cot next to him was whimpering and crying fretfully. The other children, much older than he was, were boisterously noisy and openly staring at him. There was the strong smell of disinfectant.

His disillusion was complete.

"I don't like this place. I don't want to sleep here tonight."
His eyes filled with tears.

"Darling, it will only be for two nights. You'll be home again on Friday morning, and we'll all be together again."

"It's a horrible place," he said, bursting into tears. "I don't want to stay here alone."

I appealed to the nurse in charge.

"Please let me stay with him tonight. He is so frightened. I won't disturb anyone. I'll sit quietly by his bed."

"It is not permitted," she said kindly.

He cried when I left him, and when his father came, he pierced him with the weapon of his grief.

That night we sat by the fire in silence. Our thoughts, our love, our fears were all with Nicky: thoughts that must be disciplined so they should not destroy us, fears that must be hidden so he should not see them.

We were poor company for our little son who was sitting with us, and Dirk went to bed early.

I walked into the ward at two o' clock the next afternoon. Nicky lay on his back, his eyes dark pools, his face bluish-grey with exhaustion. A faint glint lit his eyes when he saw me, then he closed them and the lashes lay darkly on his cheeks.

The baby was still crying. The other children were laughing and talking. Too drained to care about his environment, he lay with his eyes closed; I sat next to him holding his hand.

He looked better the next morning. His eyes were still heavy and smudged with fatigue, but he smiled and was pleased to see us.

I dressed him, and Bill packed his clothes and toys into a suitcase.

While we were talking to him, a nurse walked in and smiled at Bill.

"Dr. de Goede would like you to come downstairs. He will meet you at the door of the Cardiac Clinic."

Nicky's eyes widened with anxiety when he saw we were leaving him.

"Don't worry, darling," I said reassuringly. "We'll be back in ten minutes."

We took the elevator to the ground floor; when we entered the passage leading to the Cardiac Clinic we were met by a milling throng of people. We elbowed and weaved our way through them, and suddenly found ourselves face to face with Dr. de Goede.

He greeted us with a smile. He looked tired and pale.

"Let's move along and see if we can find a less crowded spot."

We followed him, once more pushing our way through the mass of people, until he stopped at the bottom of a narrow staircase where it was reasonably private.

"I worked on Nicky for nearly four hours yesterday morning. Normally a catheterization should not take more than two hours, but in his case I was unable to get the catheter into his pulmonary artery. We have just received a new machine from Sweden, and I could have switched Nicky onto it, but I felt that he had taken enough punishment: and frankly, I had taken about as much as I could stand. I went to bed afterwards."

His face was strained.

"I am afraid Nicky must have another catheterization in six months' time."

Bill suddenly sat down on the bottom step of the stairs and put his head between his knees. He sat like that for several minutes. When he looked up his face was ashen.

He smiled wanly at Dr. de Goede.

"I'm sorry. I always have this odd reaction when I get a shock."

We took Nicky home. He was pleased to be back with his brother and sisters, but for many weeks he was listless and easily tired.

Dirk was now playing tennis. In the evenings when Bill coached him, Nicky squatted at the side of the court, watching wistfully. What Dirk lacked in talent, he made up for in enthusiasm. He was convinced he would be a champion.

At Easter he entered for his first tournament.

One evening he said to me:

"Where are you going to put the cup, Mom?"

"What cup?" I asked absently.

"The cup, when I win it."

"Oh. Well, as you know, I'm rather allergic to having cups in the sitting room."

"Will you put mine in the sitting room?" he asked very seriously, looking at me with dark blue eyes.

"All right."

"Will you put it on the mantelpiece above the fireplace?" he persisted.

"Yes."

He did not even reach the semi-finals.

Downcast for a few days, he was soon diligently practicing for the Christmas Tournament, convinced he would win it.

Dot was engaged.

It was soon apparent to me she was not in love. One evening, when we were alone, I asked her suddenly: "Dot, are you in love with him?"

She wriggled uncomfortably.

"Yes," she said, in a small, flat voice.

"Are you quite sure?"

She looked embarrassed.

"Yes," she said, in the same unemotional tone.

I spoke to Bill.

"She's no more in love with that boy than I am."

"Look," he said. "You can't run other people's lives for them. We have enough to worry about as it is. Let them work things out for themselves."

Sue had grown into a tall, lovely girl. She was like a filly galloping down the road with the bit in her teeth, letting a flying kick at anyone who tried to stop her.

A strange assortment of men invaded Greystone. We quarreled from morning to night. Even Bill's good nature wore thin.

Nicky's heart was set on going to Dirk's school. He spoke of little else.

"I'm not a bit happy about it," I said to Bill. "We should send him to the Rudolph Steiner School. It's much smaller and he will practically have individual tuition. With his intelligence he should do very well there and would not be so conscious of his inability to play games or take Gym."

"I don't agree with you," Bill said firmly. "Nicky has set his heart on going to Dirk's school. He'll feel more out of things than ever if we send him to a different school."

"But they'll bully him. They will say horrible things to him about his blue lips and his round face."

"I don't think you will find that will happen. We must try and give Nicky as normal an upbringing as possible."

We took him to the school to be interviewed by the Headmaster.

He was not at all shy, answering all the questions he was asked with confidence, his eyes never leaving the master's face. He was determined to pass this test with flying colors.

He was sent outside to play.

When we were alone, we spoke of our fears, of his condition, and of our hopes for his future.

I said to the Headmaster: "I'll tell you frankly that I am not keen on Nicky coming to a big school like this in which sport plays such a large part. I am so afraid when the boys find out that Nicky is unable to play games or take Gym, they will bully him and be unkind to him."

"On the contrary, you will find the boys will be very kind to him. We have other handicapped children in this school and the boys are strongly protective towards them and always try to help them. The teacher will tell them about Nicky. Don't worry, I can assure you he will be very happy here."

But I was only partly reassured.

28

CHAPTER 6

NICKY was now five and one-half, and the time for the second catheterization was upon us. Now he was under no illusions about what was in store for him, and he tortured himself and us with his misery.

He noticed none of the sights when we drove to the hospital.

A squirrel, bounding across the road with a fir cone in its mouth, elicited no comment.

I pointed out a snow white egret perched on the rump of a grazing wildebeest. He turned his head away. He sat huddled in the car, wrapped in gloom, casting the same dark pall upon my spirits.

This time the ward was comparatively empty. We had not been there long, before Dr. de Goede walked in and greeted us warmly.

"Hello, Nicky. How are you?"

Nicky looked at him tearfully and said nothing.

"We're taking him down to the Cardiac Clinic for examination."

"Do you want me to come with him?" I asked.

Nicky cast me an anguished look.

"Yes, by all means come along!"

He was put into a wheelchair and pushed down to the Cardiac Clinic. Even this novelty failed to lift the darkness from his spirits.

He stood miserable and silent while he was being examined. When the electro-cardiograph was done, he cried silently, his eyes reproachful and accusing. I knew I must leave him. Alone, his natural pride and courage would make him pull himself together. A doctor stepped between us and gave me the opportunity of silently slipping out of the room. When I reached the car I burst into tears. I felt as though I had betrayed him.

Again Bill and I were bound together by our mutual suffering, united yet separate in our tormented thoughts and fears.

The following day I found Nicky, as before, apathetic and exhausted. Once again when we fetched him the next morning he gave us a pleased tired smile. He was impatient to go home.

"When are we leaving? Why are sitting here?"

"We're waiting for Dr. de Goede."

"Why?"

"Because he will tell us about the test he did on you."

"Why is he taking so long?"

A moment later, he walked into the ward carrying a sheaf of papers and X-ray photographs. If he had looked drawn and pale before, now he looked positively haggard.

"I think we should go onto the balcony."

I smiled at Nicky.

"We'll be back in ten minutes."

We followed him outside.

He looked through the X-ray photographs, finally selecting one.

"We worked on Nicky for a long time yesterday and were unable to find his pulmonary artery."

He showed us the X-ray photograph.

"This is where it should be." He marked the place with his finger. "As you can see, nothing is there."

I looked at the photograph; a quiver of apprehension chilled my spine.

"In most cases of Fallots Tetralogy a murmur can be heard when the blood is pumped through the narrowing. In Nicky's case I've heard no murmur. However, in cases of extreme narrowing the volume of blood passing through the stricture is so reduced that no murmur can be heard. Despite all our attempts yesterday, no pulmonary artery could be demonstrated and we've had to change the diagnosis to Pulmonary Atresia."

"What does that mean?"

"In the most extreme case the pulmonary artery is completely sealed off at its origin from the right ventricle. This is called Pulmonary Atresia. When I first saw Nicky, a murmur had been heard and Fallots Tetralogy had been diagnosed. However, when I saw him, there was no murmur even after recording with a sensitive phono-cardiograph. The object of the cardiac catheterization was to differentiate between extreme Fallots Tetralogy and Pulmonary Atresia. When we could not show up the pulmonary artery, we had to settle for Pulmonary Atresia."

"Is it operable?" I asked quickly.

He looked ill and unhappy.

"No. As yet no operation has been performed for this condition. But as you know they are making fantastic strides in cardiac surgery and there is always the hope that in time something will be discovered."

Inoperable. Never had I experienced such piercing anguish.

"What is his life expectancy?" I asked dully.

"About thirty years."

He looked so strained that even in my pain I could spare

a moment of pity for him. No doctor can afford to suffer like this, I thought. He will destroy himself.

We shook hands, and he left us. We went back to Nicky. He looked up and smiled at us when we came into the ward.

Bill took his suitcase. We each took a hand and walked down the wide corridor with him towards the elevator.

My grief rose in a wave which nearly overwhelmed me. I touched Bill's arm.

He looked at me quickly, then silently nodded.

As they stepped into the elevator, I slipped down the stairs and stopped by the window on the landing, fighting fiercely to regain control of myself.

Now was not the time for the luxury and relief of tears. Until I reached home I must hide my sorrow and despair from my small son.

I stared unseeingly into the dreary courtyard. I heard people walking up and down the stairs behind me; some of them, talking and laughing, were silent when they passed me. Slowly I regained command of myself.

When I walked out of the hospital into the bright sunshine, Bill and Nicky were standing next to the glinting pool looking at the goldfish. Bill's head was slightly on one side, as it always is when he is sad. This poignant indication of his grief pierced me like an arrow. My battle for self-control was half won.

Nicky chatted cheerfully all the way home. Now everything caught his attention: a friend passing in a car, a soaring hawk, the busy squirrels gathering their winter harvest. I was unable to join in their conversation. I sat with my back half turned to them, the tears silently streaming down my face.

The next day I wrote to Dr. de Goede.

"This is just a note to thank you for the infinite pains you have taken with Nicky.

"You had a very unenviable task having to break the bad news to us.

"We both deeply appreciate your kindness and sympathy."

32

CHAPTER 7

WE HAD to learn to live with it. It was the last thing I thought of before falling asleep, and the first thought in my mind on waking. Now I remembered what Dr. Thomas had said. "Six years is the ideal operative age. The heart is the most wonderful muscle of the body; it is able to compensate for any defect and will build up the smaller veins to take the place of those which are not functioning properly. One must operate before the compensation is too great; otherwise, the heart becomes too lopsided to make a successful operation possible."

Would something be discovered for Nicky's condition in the span of time required? Hope was ever present like a bright flame.

There was a door in my mind which was locked, bolted, and barred; sometimes in the small hours of the morning it silently swung open. How would it end? Would he have a heart attack or a stroke; or would it be a slow deterioration, a lingering death too terrible to contemplate? Sick and trembling with the horror of it, I would sit up and switch on the light, slam this imaginary door shut and bolt it again.

We could not enter a store or the smallest shop without someone commenting on his appearance.

"Why are his lips so blue?"

"Have you been eating mulberries?"

"He is purple! Is he cold?"

We took the elevator. The girl operator looked at him. "He's got something wrong with his heart, hasn't he?"

I was holding his hand and stared hard in front of me, ignoring her. Undeterred, she added, "My little sister looked just like him. She died when she was six."

They tortured him daily.

He was playing at St. James in the white sand, collecting shells and tiny orange starfish, carefully arranging them in a small translucent pool. He started to cry.

"What is wrong, Nicky?"

"That man is staring at me."

"Of course he isn't."

"He is! He is! He is!"

Not only must we learn to live with it; we also must help him to live with it. I brought it out into the open and talked about it.

"Try taking no notice when people remark that you are blue. Just think how stupid and insensitive they are."

Now, when somebody said "Have you been eating mulberries?" I nudged him, rolling my eyes expressively to the ceiling, and for a moment there was a fleeting wisp of a smile.

This constant reference to his appearance depressed his spirits far more than the knowledge that he was physically incapable of competing with other children. Often I saw him biting his lip, trying to stem his tears.

His face was moon-shaped and markedly blue. His lips, ears, and bulbous fingertips were purple; his eyes permanently bloodshot. He was spindly-legged and flat-footed. His corn colored hair was silky and unruly.

He was not at all shy. At six he was mature for his age and had great dignity for such a small boy.

An African nurse maid called Anna had looked after him from the age of two. She took a lively interest in everything that took place in our household. She expressed her opinion on Dot's engagement, Sue's men friends, Dirk's friends. The only time her good humor failed her was when Nicky was rude to her; then she became temperamental and excitable, shouting at him as loudly as he shouted at her.

He was self-willed and disobedient, and his temper was violent. If Mazeppa, the Siamese cat, unintentionally scratched him, he shouted with temper and hit him with his clenched fist. If Sarah, the boxer, accidently trod on him while he was playing on the floor, he kicked her. I was the only one who could manage him when he got into a rage. He knew I would tolerate neither his tantrums nor his rudeness. He knew the same treatment would be meted out to him as had been meted out to his brother and sisters.

"You're horrible," he would say loudly.

Nevertheless, I knew the boundaries set for his standard of behavior gave him a feeling of security.

Dirk was charming to the animals, and they loved him. Every afternoon, Sarah stood at the gate waiting for him to return from school. As soon as she saw him, she ran down the road to greet him joyfully. She followed him wherever he went and lay curled at his feet when he did his homework.

The day arrived when Nicky walked into my room and stood in front of the long mirror, admiring himself with a pleased smile. He was wearing his new school clothes. The navy blue cap accentuated the roundness of his face; the blazer, the blueness of his lips. He looked small, frail, and pathetic.

Dirk, who was skinny and not tall for his age, stood behind him inspecting himself critically.

35

"Mom, you must speak to Nicky. I told him he mustn't show off at school, and he just says 'Oh shurrup.' "

"Nicky, Dirk is quite right."

"Oh Mom! Of course I won't show off. Dirk makes me sick!"

They bickered all the way to school. Dirk was mostly to blame. He teased him incessantly, delighting in his violent displays of temper, and now Nicky was unbearably cheeky to him.

"I'll take Nicky in, Mom," Dirk said. "I know where he has to go."

"Do you want to go with Dirk, or do you want to go with me?" I asked.

"I'll go with Dirk," he said quickly.

He had no objections when Dirk took his hand. I sat in the car and watched them walk slowly down the path and disappear into the school building. Now he was on his own. I could no longer protect him from the world. I was waiting for him when he walked out of the school at quarter past twelve.

"How was school?" I asked fearfully.

"Fine. It's a very nice school."

We were to find the prophecies made by the headmaster coming true. The boys in Nicky's class protected him and loved him. They never commented on his appearance. There were boys in the higher classes who called him 'old blue lips,' 'old purple lips' or 'old black lips,' but his own class was loyal and staunch.

I said to him once, "Has any boy in your class ever teased you about being blue?"

"Not a single boy," he said proudly. "The other day a Standard Two boy came up to me and said 'You stupid old purple lips' and Maxwell swiped him as hard as he could."

They asked him to their parties. He went to more parties in a year than Dot, Sue, and Dirk put together.

Every morning a friend waited for him at the school gate. As soon as Bill stopped the car, he darted forward, opened the

36

door, took Nicky's suitcase and carried it for him. Sometimes three little boys stood waiting. The first one carried his suitcase, the second took his cap, the third took his hymn book out of his blazer pocket and opened it to the correct page.

He called them all by their surnames, unlike his brother. They could so easily have broken him. Instead, they built up his confidence and his self-respect. They helped him as we could never do. We were aware that the guidance and kindness was directed by the staff and parents who knew of the terrible sentence passed on him, and they did much to lighten our burden.

We saw little of Dot and Sue at this time. They were at the art school all day and out every night.

Every year I did a new piece of construction in the garden. It took 18 months to clear the bush, level the ground, and plant the long lawn, which now ends with a woodbine hedge and an archway. I scrapped the untidy sloping lawn next to the house, built it up, and planted a covert of rhododendrons and hydrangeas underneath the oak tree. Azaleas were planted around the ancient wild laurel.

My father had persuaded me to plant six avocado pear trees in our garden. Now the trees were tall and lush, and each year, heavily laden with fruit.

That year, the courtyard was paved behind the house. I placed the swing-seat beneath the oak tree we had brought up from Hohenort and made a three-foot bed, with a low white wall, covering it with potted plants. Fuchsias, begonias, impatience, and cymbidium orchids flourished in the dappled shade. Dirk brought me ferns to plant in the stone wall. In the summer, opulent purple achemene dripped from the hanging basket.

It was cool and sheltered, and on the hot summer days we sat there, seldom setting foot in the house.

CHAPTER 8

THE following year Dot and Sue were working, determined to save money to have a trip overseas. I did everything to encourage them.

Our friends were unfailingly kind to Nicky. Whenever we had guests, the two small boys were allowed to sit with us until dinner was served. When the guests arrived, they stood near the door waiting to shake hands; Nicky was warmly greeted, hugged, and kissed; Dirk, unwittingly, was sometimes overlooked. Often a rand or a two-rand note was pressed into Nicky's hand. His money box was overflowing with cash, which he never failed to gloatingly count in front of his brother.

In spite of his difficult position in the family, Dirk's good nature remained unimpaired, and he was full of confidence.

At school, Dirk kept a brotherly eye on Nicky, and his friends greeted Nicky and spoke to him if they saw him in the playground.

When I fetched them at school, Dirk always carried Nicky's suitcase. One afternoon when we arrived at Greystones and Dirk had just stepped out of the car, Nicky, who was still sitting on the back seat, shouted in a hectoring tone:

"Dirk! My bag!"

I put my arm over the back of the seat, turned around, and looked at him.

"What do you mean 'Dirk! My bag!'? He doesn't have to carry your bag. You are quite capable of carrying it yourself—and I've never ever heard you thank him. Now that we are on the subject, I've never ever heard you thank any of your friends either, and often you don't even say good-by to them. Just remember not to take other people's kindness for granted."

He looked at me with his mouth slightly open and remained silent. The next day when his friend opened the door of the car and placed his bag inside, he said "Thanks, Dent."

When Nicky had his party, Dirk organized everything. He arranged target-shooting with his pellet gun, cricket on the tennis court. He thought of games in which Nicky could participate and succeeded in keeping the mass of small boys in a homogeneous group.

Dot and Sue booked their passage on the *Athlone Castle*. Greystones was in a turmoil before their departure. They were always out, and packed in fits and starts, turning the whole house upside down. Bedrooms were chaotic; clothes lay on the floor, the chairs, and their beds.

Dirk and Nicky became affected with the suppressed excitement of their sisters and were as animated as they were when the day arrived.

Dot's fiancé, the picture of gloom, was unable to bring himself to see her off.

Anna said:

"Madam must take me to the ship to say good-by to Miss Dot and Miss Sue."

They said good-by to Sarah, who was wagging her tail

but not looking happy. Sue said good-by to Frikkie, a little black pomeranian, a gift from a boy friend. They said good-by to Mazeppa, the Siamese cat, to the ginger cat, and the grey cat. We packed the luggage into the two cars, locked the house, and our entire ménage set out for the Cape Town docks.

The band was playing, the ship streaming with bunting, and the decks milling with thousands of people.

Dot, Sue, and a friend shared a cabin, and we all walked down to the bowels of the ship to inspect it, literally forcing our way through the dense crowd of people. By the time we had fought our way back to the lounge, I was suffering from claustrophobia, sore feet, and a headache. We huddled into a small group in the corner, hemmed in by a thousand people. As always at such times, our conversation became spasmodic and strained.

We were all relieved when the bells rang and we had to leave. We kissed them and hugged them, feeling close to tears. Bill picked up Nicky and I took Dirk's hand. Pushed and jostled, we made our way down the crowded gangway. We stood on the quay looking up at the great ship, our eyes scanning the crowded decks trying to find them.

"There they are!" Bill cried. He waved, and they waved back at us. Dot was radiant. I nudged Bill.

"No girl who is leaving her fiancé for six months has any business to look as happy as that."

He grinned broadly.

Anna had joined us. The band played Auld Lang Syne. As the ship slowly moved from the quay, Anna started to wail.

"Ooh-la! Ooh-la! Ooh-la!"

"Anna," I said. "Why on earth are you crying?"

The tears were streaming down her cheeks.

"Ooh-la! We never see Miss Dot and Miss Sue again."

We drove through the docks and across the common, and parked on the grass in front of the Green Point lighthouse. We sat in the car, watching the ship slowly steaming towards the pale horizon.

I whispered a silent "Good luck."

"Ooh-la," Anna wailed. "Ooh-la."

CHAPTER 9

GREYSTONES seemed very quiet after they were gone. I missed Dot's companionship, and the excitement Sue brought into our lives. Dirk and Nicky missed them even more. Every weekend in the summer they had gone to the beach with Dot and her fiancé or Sue and her latest swain. Dirk, thin as he was, had stayed in the water for hours or run along the beach with Sarah. Nicky played on the sand near the water's edge; occasionally he stood knee deep and immersed his body in the cold sea. His heart was set on learning how to swim.

"I'm sure it is one of the few things he will be able to do," I said to Bill.

"You don't think that it will be too much for him?"

"I don't think so. If he can learn to float and do the dog-paddle, it will make life so much safer for him. Now, if he should fall into one of our friends' swimming pools, he would drown."

"Well," Bill said reluctantly, "take him to the swimming class and see what happens."

When the summer term started, I fetched him at the preparatory school one Tuesday morning and drove him to the swimming pool of the high school, a quarter of a mile away. As we passed his class walking in an orderly line, they shouted and waved to him.

I helped him undress, and he proudly drew on his new bathing trunks. He stood in a row with the other boys, looking pathetically weak and blue. One by one, they were helped down the steps by the swimming instructress, until they were in a long line, holding onto the bar which ran along the edge of the pool. She demonstrated to them how to kick. I never took my eyes off him.

After ten minutes, I walked over and said to the instructress:

"Will you please lift him up."

As she did so, I took his hands and pulled him out of the water. He looked terrible. His face was bluish grey, his teeth were chattering, and his breathing was distressed. I took him to the changing room and dried him.

"My heart is sore," he said, pressing his hands to his chest.

Nauseous with anxiety, I bitterly reproached myself. I carried him to the car, and drove back to the schoolroom to fetch his suitcase.

"You won't be able to take swimming lessons, Nicky, it will be too much for you."

"Yes, I know."

"Is your heart still hurting you?"

"Yes, it's still a bit sore, but it's not so bad now."

There was a pause.

"Will I one day be like other boys? Will I one day look different?"

It was as though he had plunged a dagger into my heart.

"Darling, Dad, the doctors, and I are trying all the time to

44

find something to help you. One day we hope they will do an operation which will make you just like other boys."

He said nothing.

When we arrived home, I told Anna to make tea, and we sat together and drank it in the dappled shade of the courtyard.

Nicky came down with a mild attack of mumps. Any illness was cause for alarm, alarm deeply shared by our family doctor, who was also Nicky's godfather. Over the years he had watched over Nicky as though he were his own son, often dropping in casually to reassure himself that all was well.

Absence from school had little effect on Nicky, who maintained his position near the top of his class. He was an interested, talkative, and naughty pupil.

Dirk started the year somewhere near the bottom of his class, and slowly worked his way up until by the end of the year he had improved his position sufficiently to be awarded a prize for perseverance. This small success gave him much pleasure.

"Why does Dirk get a prize when he only came fifteenth? I came third," said Nicky.

"We all know where you came—you never stop telling us."

"Well, I don't think it's fair."

He was ambitious to be first in his class.

When his school report arrived at the end of the year, it was obvious he was deeply disappointed to read he was still third. His teacher wrote: "Nicky is much too talkative."

He snorted with disgust and flung his report across the room.

"She makes me sick! She's always saying that."

Letters arrived regularly from Dot and Sue. At first they were desperately homesick, but soon they settled down, finding their new life exciting and full of interest.

Within a few months I received a letter from Dot.

45

"I have discovered I'm not in love with him. What must I do?"

I wrote back by return post.

"Break it off!"

We often saw her fiancé. I knew in time he would forget her and find great happiness with someone else.

CHAPTER 10

THE clouds were darkening on our horizon. In the early postwar years, the family business of Wm. Spilhaus & Co. Ltd. passed through a prosperous period. This state of affairs, however, began to change in the middle 1950's. Over the years, the business had been lulled into a sense of false security. The necessary steps to counteract the downward trend were often discussed but not diligently carried out. Soon, to the concern of the Board and shareholders, losses began to take the place of the profits previously enjoyed, and the family, who constituted the majority shareholding in the firm, found themselves deprived of any income from their capital investment in the Company.

This development was a crippling blow to us. Bill was a large shareholder, and we now found ourselves deprived of an income which we had always taken for granted. The hope was always with us that an operation would be found to help Nicky, and for this purpose we tried to save something each year to enable us to meet the vast expense such an operation would entail. Now we found we could not save, nor were we able to make ends meet.

At the beginning of the new year, Bill said to me one evening:

"We can't go on like this. We will have to do something drastic."

"What do you suggest?"

He was looking very tired.

"I've been thinking about it for a long time. If we let Greystones and lived in a hotel for 18 months or two years, we would be able to save and straighten out our affairs."

"Surely we couldn't save living in a hotel."

"It would cost half what it costs us to live at the moment. First, we would receive a steady income from the letting of Greystones; second, if I could arrange suitable terms with a hotel, it would cost infinitely less than it does now with two servants, a gardener, and all the expense involved in running a home."

"Have you a hotel in mind?"

"Yes. I thought we might stay at Hohenort."

Hohenort! Grandfather Spilhaus' old home, which was now a hotel. There was a slight lightening of my depression. We would be close to Greystones; Dirk could continue to roam through the woods and explore the streams. We could maintain strong ties with the old house.

The next evening Bill drove down to Hohenort to interview the manager.

When he walked into the sitting room an hour later, he looked less strained.

"Well, everything is arranged. The manager agreed to the terms I suggested. We should be quite comfortable and I have arranged that we will occupy Mom's old room. They have now partitioned it off into two rooms; the one is quite a reasonable

48

size and has its own bathroom. The other partition I thought was too small for the boys, so they will go into Dad's old dressing room, which will be only two doors away."

"When will we go there?"

"I have arranged for us to move in on the first of March. We will now have to start doing something about Greystones."

I love Greystones. It was built when we were very young and originally designed to accommodate a family of four. We always intended enlarging it to make it more comfortable, but after Nicky was born, all plans for alterations were shelved.

The dining room is cramped, the bedrooms too small; there is only one bathroom. We stand on the cold southern slopes of Wynberg Hill; in the winter months we shiver, exposed to the full fury of the northwest gales.

Perched as we are on the knuckle of the hill with the valley lying at our feet, looking across to the sea and into the infinite horizon beyond, we have a feeling of peace, of complete freedom I have never experienced elsewhere. Here too the air is different, fresh, sweet, and untainted.

It was not easy for me to accept the idea of someone else living at Greystones.

My feelings were nebulous, unreasonable, and basically jealous.

A few days later Bill telephoned me.

"A man will be coming to see Greystones at twelve o' clock this morning. Will you make a point of being there when he arrives?"

I was on the lawn when he parked his streamlined, expensive car next to the magnolia tree. He was sleek, well fed and opulent. He introduced himself, and we shook hands.

"You're wasting your time," I said.

"What do you mean?" he said, straightening a rich silk tie.

"This isn't what you are looking for. It's a cramped, small cottage, and damned inconvenient."

That evening I said to Bill:

49

"I couldn't bear to think of him living at Greystones."

"You're mad," he said aghast. "You can't put people off like that, just because you don't like them. You can't hand pick the people who will stay there. You must be businesslike."

"I loathe showing people around the house. They seem to think that because a house is to let, it entitles them to make disparaging remarks. It has an unfortunate effect on me; I become cold and distant, and practically throw them out."

"Look," he said firmly. "You must let me handle this."

A week later the house was rented to a couple whom we instantly liked.

They insisted that we continue to play tennis at Greystones on Saturday afternoons.

"And we would like you to continue working in your garden," she added. "Whenever you feel like it."

So Greystones was not entirely lost to us, and we gained two new friends.

Our house is small. Nevertheless, it was remarkable how much junk we had accumulated over the last 20 years. Clothes, books and toys had to be discarded with a ruthless disregard for sentiment.

Bill and the boys undermined my efforts.

"You can't throw this away," Bill said, picking up a derelict hat. "This is my favorite fishing hat."

"Good Lord!" in an outraged voice. "You weren't thinking of getting rid of this!"

"Dad! Look what Mom wants to throw away!"

"Oh. I've been looking for this everywhere. Where did you find it?"

They exasperated me beyond endurance.

I told Anna we were leaving.

"Will you work for us again, when we come back to Greystones?"

"Yes, Madam."

Like a frightened bird, she fled at once to a new home, finding me a good natured placid girl to take her place for the last month.

Bill always comes home for lunch on Friday. Nicky and I sat on the swing seat in the courtyard waiting for him. A man appeared at the wall, clearing his throat.

"Excuse me, Madam. I knocked your dog with my milk van."

"When did it happen?"

"Now, Madam."

"Did you knock her, or did your van go over her?"

"I'm sorry, Madam. I go over her. Then she ran away."

With a sinking heart I called Harold, the gardener, and we searched through the garden trying to find Sarah.

Bill joined us ten minutes later. We could find her nowhere. It was like looking for a needle in a haystack. We had almost given up hope when Harold shouted that he had found her in the woods at the bottom of the garden.

"I can't go with you," I said to Bill. "I'll wait here."

Nicky started to follow him.

"You stay with me, Nicky."

"Why?"

"Because I tell you to," I said.

Bill was gone only a few minutes. I watched him walk up the steps and cross the lawn towards us, his head slightly on one side.

"How is she?"

"I've come to fetch my revolver. She's internally injured, and dying in agony. I will have to shoot her."

Bill looked tired and worn when he rejoined us.

"I've told Harold to bury her. Shame. Poor Dirk."

"I know. I'm dreading having to tell him."

I sat on the bench under the silver birch tree, waiting for him to return from school, trying to think of the gentlest way of telling him his love was dead.

He took the short cut through the wild garden, past the

beacon-topped boulder and walked down the steps, carrying his cap in one hand and his suitcase in the other. I stood up.

"Dirk!" Nicky shouted. "The milkman drove over Sarah, and Dad shot her dead."

He stopped in his tracks as though struck. His face whitened, and his eyes filled with tears.

"Why?" he asked with quivering lips.

"And Harold has buried her," Nicky added loudly.

"Keep quiet!" I shouted at him.

"But why did Dad shoot her?" Dirk asked. The tears were now pouring down his cheeks. It was the first time I had seen him cry for years.

"He had to shoot her, darling. She was in terrible pain."

"But she might have got better. Why did he kill her?"

"She could never get better, Dirk. It was a dreadful thing for your poor father to have to do. He loved Sarah almost as much as you do."

He turned away and walked into the house.

Nicky was smiling widely.

"Aren't you sorry for poor Sarah and Dirk?" I asked furiously.

"Of course I am," he said with surprised indignation.

The painters moved into the house, and we were living under chaotic conditions. Furniture was moved into the center of the rooms. Half-packed trunks and suitcase were stacked in the bedrooms, and everywhere the pervading smell of paint.

CHAPTER 11

THREE days later, at half past six, we locked the back-door of Greystones. It was now a cold, empty shell, and we were glad to leave it. We drove down to Hohenort in the two cars. I took Dirk, Mazeppa and Frikkie. Bill and Nicky traveled down in the big car, which was stacked with coats, dressing gowns, tennis rackets, golf clubs, and clothes which we had been unable to pack into our suitcases.

The grey cat and the ginger cat were remaining at Greystones.

"You may leave the two cats with us," said Gill, our new tenant, "but not the Siamese cat. That voice would drive us mad."

Bill had taken me down to Hohenort a few days previously to inspect our rooms. I was unutterably depressed when I saw the hideous, ostentatious furniture, the stained carpet, the unattractive bedspreads, and the monstrous dressing table.

"Can't we ask them to remove these monstrosities and bring in our divans, a few pieces of our own furniture, and try to make this look more like a sitting room?" I asked.

"I think that is an excellent idea. I will speak to the manager."

Now the only piece of hotel furniture which remained was a cheap, inadequate wardrobe. My Queen Anne writing desk stood next to the window. A large Persian carpet from our sitting room covered the dirty beige carpet. Our two divans took the place of the two large ostentatious beds. We had sent down two chairs, occasional tables, pictures and *objets d'art*.

When we entered our room that evening, the pictures and ornaments were piled on the divans, the suitcases pushed against the wardrobe, and the furniture scattered haphazardly around the room. It was chaotic and depressing.

A vase of flowers, with a note attached, stood on my desk, a touching gesture from two friends who knew in what low spirits we would be this night.

Dirk and Nicky were happy; for them it was the beginning of a new, exciting life.

The next morning, while the boys were at school, I achieved some semblance of order in the two rooms where we were to spend the next 18 months. I pushed the two divans against the wall. Later I was to buy bright covers and cushions, and a screen to hide the wash basin. I placed the chairs and tables, put out the pieces of porcelain and silver, and hung the pictures. It was still a hotel room, but now it was no longer so coldly impersonal, and it was redeemed by the two great sash windows. Looking out across the vines to the white sand dunes and the deep blue sea, we had an intimate and beautiful view of the Constantia Valley. On the right was the feathery bar of a formal row of Lombardy poplars and to the left a wood of fine old oaks. We had a small bathroom, with a barn door next to it, which opened onto a wide, sunny balcony overlooking the neglected garden. Here I placed a sandbox for Mazeppa, the Siamese cat, who was in a state of slinking abject misery.

We soon settled down to our new way of life.

Hohenort Hotel was run by two young men who had been educated at one of the leading schools in Cape Town. Between them, they succeeded in creating an informal and pleasant atmosphere and the food was good. There was a certain sadness staying at Hohenort. The big house had lost the graciousness and intimacy of the past; it was filled with memories of Grandfather and the warm-hearted family who had lived with him. Now it had the neglected air of an unloved woman. Soon after we moved in, Bill noticed that his cigars were disappearing. He suspected the boy who vacuumed our carpets.

"He's pinching my cigars," said Bill. "Every time I open the box, another one is missing."

As winter set in and the northwest gales started sweeping down the valley, fires were lit each evening in the big fireplace, so the entrance into the hotel at this time always appeared warm and welcoming. At that time of the year only a handful of people resided in the hotel, and we soon became acquainted with them. There was the genial British major, who sat in the hall like a fat, generous spider, trying to waylay whoever was walking past; quite willing to buy a drink for anyone who would listen to his reminiscences.

There was the gay divorceé, with high piled hair, who had a flaxen-haired daughter named Rachel. Rachel was two years older than Nicky and soon had him completely in her thrall. She was naughty and adventurous. He was utterly enchanted by her, and they became inseparable. Often I searched all over the big house trying to find them.

One evening I walked into our room and was surprised to find our bathroom door locked. I banged on the door.

"Who's in there?" I shouted.

"Me," said Nicky.

"Why have you locked the door?"

"Rachel and I are having a bath."

"Open the door at once!"

The room was clouded with steam; the bath was filled to the brim with soap suds, and water was seeping underneath the door. I scolded them roundly and dried Nicky's hair, which was plastered to his head like a smooth cap. When they were both dressed, I made them clean the bath and mop up the water. Future communal bathing was forbidden.

Every evening before dinner Dirk came and sat with us in our room. Frikkie lay stretched in front of the heater, and Mazeppa was curled in a ball on the divan.

"Where is Nicky?"

"He and Rachel are playing a very childish game in the passage, and they are making a lot of noise."

"Tell him to come and sit with us."

Ten minutes later Nicky walked into the room.

"May Rachel come in too?"

Sometimes I was hard-hearted.

"Not tonight. Tell Rachel to go and sit with her mother."

Then he glowered and sulked.

"It's boring in here. There's nothing to do."

"Get a book and read."

"I don't feel like reading."

"Fetch your coloring book or playing cards."

"I don't feel like it."

Muttering under his breath, morose and fidgety, he disturbed the harmony in our room. Whether it was Rachel's influence or whether it was due to his different environment and new mode of life, I was finding him increasingly difficult to handle. He was becoming disobedient, naughty, and often deceitful.

During the morning while the boys were at school, I occupied myself in the neglected hotel garden. I pruned the unkempt old roses, brought fuchsias, impatience and begonias from Greystones and planted them in the shade beneath the wall. I showed the two gardeners how to construct a balustraded wall.

Sometimes I slipped up to Greystones and pruned the roses and hydrangeas, often bringing back a camellia or a sprig of azaleas.

Frikkie went everywhere with me. He was a highly intelligent little dog, with a foxlike face and small, dark brown luminous eyes. I had trained him to walk at my heels through dense traffic. He sat at the door of the store, waiting for me while I did my shopping; he followed me everywhere like a shadow.

One morning I found Nicky with a slight temperature. I thought it advisable to phone his godfather, our family doctor.

"I'm quite certain Nicky has flu, but I'd like you to drop in and see him while you are on your morning round."

Nicky always wept pathetically whenever he had to remain in bed.

"I'll go down now and buy you a coloring book and some crayons," I said to console him. "There are quite a few things to do, so I won't be back before eleven o'clock."

However, having bought them, I impulsively decided to return to Hohenort immediately. Nicky was not in his room. I walked into our bedroom and found him lying on his father's bed in his dressing gown. His eyes were closed, and between his lips was a half-smoked cigar. From his blissful expression and evident enjoyment, it was obvious that he was a confirmed cigar smoker. A pall of silvery pungent smoke filled the room.

He was appalled when he opened his eyes and saw me. He removed the cigar from between his lips, his eyes widened, and his mouth fell open in consternation.

"You naughty boy! That's what has been happening to Dad's cigars. I've a good mind to spank you."

Hurriedly, I pushed open the barn door and escaped onto the balcony, trying to smother the hysterical laughter I was unable to control.

A few evenings later I said to him:

"Well, Nicky, Dad and I have been wondering for some time what to give you for Christmas, and I've thought of the perfect present."

"What?" he asked, his face brightly alive with interest.

"A box of cigars."

His face fell, and his lower lip trembled.

"I don't want cigars."

"But you love smoking cigars. You'll be able to smoke one whenever you feel like it."

He burst into tears.

"I don't want cigars," he wailed.

Bill could stand it no longer.

"Shame. Mom's only teasing you, Nicky."

That was the last cigar he ever smoked.

Letters arrived regularly from Dot and Sue. They were both now working for the same firm in London and excitedly making plans to spend a holiday in Austria.

The news of Sarah's death and our move to Hohenort had depressed them both deeply.

"I felt like crying," Sue wrote.

But Bill's plan was working. We were now saving and setting our house in order.

CHAPTER 12

Whenspring came to the Cape, the hotel filled
up rapidly. Visitors arrived from overseas and
from all over South Africa. Every day we saw new faces and
family groups. With this influx of humanity, a certain intimacy
and warmth vanished from Hohenort, and it became a typical
hotel.

The country was beautiful. Acres and acres of blue or yellow agricultural lupins stirred gently in the soft breeze. The
pastures were green and lush. The fruit trees burgeoned with
blossom, carpeting the grass beneath them with pink petals. Pro-
tea and leucadendron flowered on the mountain slopes. The
sides of the road were brilliantly strewn with white and yellow
daisies. The long range of the Hottentot's Holland Mountains
were deeply blue in the crisp sparkling air.

In the Peninsula the oaks burst into tender green. The fields
and the wood in my garden were dotted with clumps of white

Arum lilies. The lakes and pools were covered with small white sweetly-scented waterlilies.

The crowded hotel oppressed us. Every Sunday we took a picnic basket and drove into the country. As the weather became warmer, we spent the day on the white-hot beaches of the Peninsula, Frikkie accompanying us wherever we went.

We were delighted at this time to receive an invitation from my brother, Paul, to spend a weekend with them at Still Bay. Everything was packed and we went to bed early, excited at the prospect of escaping from the hotel for a few days. At two o' clock, I woke to find the light on. Dirk was standing at the doorway in his pajamas, his face pinched with anxiety.

"Nicky's not well."

Bill's reactions on being awakened are infinitely quicker than mine. In a flash he was out of bed, flinging on his dressing gown and quickly following Dirk out of the room.

I was fastening the cord of my own gown when he returned, carrying Nicky, who was crying piteously, in his arms.

"What's wrong?" I asked.

His face tense, he did not answer me. He put Nicky into his bed and drew up the blankets.

"Lie down, darling."

A second later Nicky sat up and gave a piercing scream of agony, clutching his chest with rigid hands.

"It's sore! It's sore!"

I was paralyzed with shock, frozen into numb immobility.

As suddenly as it had happened, it was over. He sank back, turned on his side and shut his eyes. His eyelashes fluttered and slowly his breathing became regular.

We stood together at the end of his bed, watching him, bound together in our mutual agony, yet, in our despair, unable to speak to each other.

Quarter of an hour later he started up, his eyes wide and staring, once again clutching his chest in anguish.

60

"It's sore! It's sore!"

"I'm going to wake up the manager," I said in a trembling voice. "We must phone the doctor."

Nicky had fallen back on his pillow, turned on his side, and shut his eyes.

"No, wait. He's asleep now. If he doesn't wake up again, let us leave it until the morning."

He took off his dressing gown and crept into bed beside Nicky, putting an arm gently around him. Though the night was hot, I was shivering uncontrollably. Switching off the light, I crawled into bed and lay staring into the darkness. At six o'clock his agonized screams went through me like a knife.

I jumped out of bed and pulled on my dressing gown.

"I am going to wake up the manager."

This time Bill made no attempt to stop me.

I was halfway down the stairs when he shouted:

"Come back!"

I stopped and looked back.

"Why?"

"Come back."

He was standing at the top of the stairs and to my amazement he was smiling. When I joined him, he took my arm and pressed it warmly.

"When you left the room, Nicky seized hold of the lobes of my ears, pulled my head down until my left ear was level with his mouth, and whispered 'Dad, I swallowed a tiddly-winks last night.' "

"What!"

"Yes. It's now obviously stuck in his chest."

Such a wave of relief swept over me, I nearly burst into tears.

"We must give him some dry bread to eat," I said tremulously. "We may be able to find a piece in the kitchen."

"I'll go and see if I can find some."

Five minutes later he was back with a piece of stale white bread.

I took it and broke off a small piece.

"Sit up, Nicky, and eat this."

He looked at the dry unappetizing piece of bread, wrinkling his nose fastidiously.

"I don't want to."

"If you don't eat that piece of bread immediately," I said fiercely, "I'll punish you." He could see I meant it. Still shaking from the unbearable tension, I was now unreasonably furious with him.

He reluctantly put it into his mouth, slowly chewed it with distaste, and with an effort swallowed it.

We watched him with bated breath.

He looked up with a smile.

"It's gone."

We took him back to his own bed, tucked him in, and he immediately fell soundly asleep.

When we returned to our room I said to Bill:

"That was an utter nightmare. I thought he was having a heart attack."

"Yes," he said. "I thought it was the beginning of the end."

We left for Still Bay at half past twelve.

Letters from the girls continued to come. A letter arrived from Dot.

"I've fallen in love. I can't eat and I can't sleep. It's like a sickness."

I wrote back.

"Who is he? What does he do?"

A few weeks later she wrote.

"He is a Rhodesian. He has no job at the moment and has come over here to see Europe. Whenever he needs any money he works as a waiter for a week or two."

Sue was in love with an Israeli.

I said to Bill:

"Dot may not be able to eat or sleep because she is so much in love. I can't eat or sleep because I am so worried about both of them. We should never have let them go overseas."

"You'll achieve nothing by worrying about them. They are grown up and must work out their own salvation. We can write and try to guide them. Beyond that, there is nothing more we can do."

Nicky continued to develop slowly. He put on weight and grew taller. His face became perceptibly rounder and bluer, and his fingertips heavily clubbed. He was happy at school and still maintained his third place in the class.

He often went out for the day with Rachel and her mother. A young couple came to live at Hohenort and they had a daughter called Phoebe. A little younger than Nicky, she was gentle and feminine, and whenever Rachel was out, he played with her. Whatever previous aversion he may have had for small girls had now vanished.

"Nicky says he's kissed Rachel," Dirk told us.

CHAPTER 13

Nɪᴄᴋʏ and I went to see Anna, who was cook-general for a couple who lived close to us. "Anna, we return to Greystones at the beginning of September. Will you come back to us?"

She smiled.

"Yes please, Madam."

"Have you learned to cook some nice new dishes since you've been here?"

"Na. This Madam is not fussy like Madam." There was a pause. "It is not nice to work for someone who is not fussy."

"Well, Anna. We'll all be together soon. I've had a letter from Miss Dot. She will be back with us next month, and I'm hoping that Miss Sue will be with us before long."

Dot wrote.

"Mervyn leaves for Liberia in three weeks. He will work

there for six months in order to save money so we can get married. I'm coming home after he leaves,"

It was now April, the first northwest gales were heralding the coming winter, and the hotel was once again empty. We had no difficulty booking the room next to ours for Dot. We were all excited at the prospect of seeing her soon.

The following weekend, the weather was fine and on Sunday we drove to Hout Bay to spend the morning at the beach. Frikkie sat on my lap in the circle of my arms, something which he never previously permitted.

I softly stroked his silky fur.

"I've never known him to be so affectionate," I said to Bill.

That afternoon they telephoned us at the club where we were playing tennis to tell us he was sick. Bill drove back to Hohenort immediately; by the time he arrived, poor Frikkie was dead. I was heartbroken. He had been my daily companion ever since we had come to Hohenort.

"I think he knew he was about to die. He had never shown me such affection before. I really loved him. It is the last time I'll ever place myself in a position to suffer like this. I'll never have another little dog. Never again!"

I missed him desperately.

The following week we drove to the Cape Town docks to meet Dot.

"When I saw you, Dad, Dirk and Nicky, I got a big lump in my throat," she said.

She looked well and radiantly happy. She immediately fitted into the family as though she had never left us.

"What are Sue's plans, Dot? When does she intend coming back?"

"Nathan finishes his course next month. He has applied for a temporary job in Pretoria. He is first going to Israel and is very keen that Sue should go with him, as he wants his parents to meet her. He is determined to marry her."

"What is he like?"

66

She hesitated.

"He is rather cold and ambitious. Sue needs someone much warmer. I don't think she will be happy with him."

"What should we do?" I asked Bill.

"Nothing," he said. "If you try to influence her, it will be the most certain way of making her marry him."

"By the way," I said casually. "I see someone in Durbanville has a little black pomeranian for sale."

"Buy him, Mom!" Nicky shouted.

"Yes, go on, Mom," Dirk said.

Bill was grinning.

"I thought you said you would never have another little dog."

"I know I did, but I could not realize what a gap Frikkie would leave in my life. I can't tell you how much I miss him."

"Come on, Dad," the boys shouted simultaneously.

The next day we drove to Durbanville and bought him.

He was a completely round ball of soft black fur from which emerged a pointed, silky muzzle. He looked like a tiny, woolly hedgehog, and I called him Toby.

The following week we received a letter from Sue.

"Nathan got the job he applied for in Pretoria. He wants me to meet his parents, so I will be spending ten days in Israel. We fly down to Pretoria on the twentieth of July. Aunt Marjorie has kindly offered to put us up for the weekend. I'll fly down to Cape Town on Monday morning. How I am longing to see all of you."

I said to Bill:

"I think I'll give her a surprise and drive up to Pretoria and fetch her."

"That's not your only reason." He smiled. "You want to meet Nathan."

"You're quite right."

My mother-in-law accompanied me on the thousand-mile drive to Pretoria, delighted to have this unexpected opportunity of seeing her daughter Marjorie. The drive through the hot Karoo was exhausting and I was grateful when we reached the hotel where we spent the night. The sun had set, and it was already freezingly cold. After a hot bath I joined my mother-in-law in front of a great blazing fire. We had an excellent meal, washed down with a good bottle of claret.

We left early the next morning. The Free State was bare, brown, and barren as far as the eye could see. It was already dark when we stopped in front of Marjorie's home. She was at the door to welcome us.

"I'm afraid the surprise has fallen flat. Ben's father let the cat out of the bag and Sue knows you are coming to fetch her."

A moment later Sue came running down the stairs and embraced me.

She was thinner, elegant, and good to look at.

We all went into the sitting room and sat down in front of a crackling fire. My brother-in-law, Ben, poured me a whisky and soda, and when he sank down next to me, I said softly:

"Where's the boy friend?"

He grinned.

"Ever since he heard the news that you were coming to fetch Sue, he has shut himself in his room. I think he's sitting up there biting his nails."

An hour later Nathan came into the room. I knew Sue would never marry him.

The next morning I went to tea with a friend whom I had not seen for many years. As I was leaving she said:

"What do you think of my dog?"

A gold and white boxer was lying curled in the sun.

"He is beautiful."

"Don't you want him?"

"Do you think I'm mad?" I said, rather rudely. "We've just ordered a collie-kelpie which will arrive at Greystones the day after we settle in. Bill will have a fit if I bring home another dog. What is his name?"

"Ryk. He's only two. He is a magnificent dog. His grandfather was the champion of Germany. I've been transferred, and I'm trying to find a home for him."

I walked over to him.

"Hello, Ryk," I said.

He looked up at me and wrinkled his face in a smile. It was irresistible.

"I'll take him," I said impulsively. "I'll give him to Dirk."

Early the next morning, we set out on our return to Cape Town. Ryk sat in the back of the car with Sue. I stopped frequently on the journey, taking him for short walks, but he never once relieved himself.

"How do you like Nathan, Mom?" Sue asked me suddenly.

"It is impossible for me to express any opinion, Sue; after all, I hardly know him." I was learning. Before I would have unhesitatingly expressed my opinion; now I was trying to handle it Bill's way.

When we reached Colesberg in the evening, I took Ryk for a walk down the main road of the village, introducing him to every lamp post. All to no avail. He thirstily drank the water I gave him, and ravenously gulped down a great bowl of meat. He was to spend the night in Bill's car, which was cozily housed in a large garage. I took him for a walk before I went to bed. Nothing happened.

"I've never known anything so frustrating," I said to my mother-in-law. "I shudder to think what Bill's car will be like tomorrow morning."

I was dressed and in the garage at five o' clock the next morning. He was delighted to see me. His soft velvety pushed-up face wrinkled with smiles. I was too late. Hours too late. For many weeks there were bitter complaints about the awful smell.

Toby was violently jealous of this new addition to our family. If Ryk so much as looked at me, he flew at him, a tiny ball of black fur, snapping and snarling.

Dirk was delighted to own a dog once more. He disappeared for hours with Ryk, introducing him to the woods, streams, and the secret paths of Hohenort.

I was particularly anxious to have Nicky back in a normal environment, once more in the close circle of family life. At the hotel he had had too much freedom, and I was finding it increasingly difficult to control him. He was often moody, petulant, and impertinent, due I am sure to a subconscious feeling of insecurity.

During our sojourn at Hohenort, our friends were unfailingly kind to us, inviting us regularly to dinner and to their homes, knowing at this time we could do little to return their hospitality. We were ever conscious of their deep sympathy.

Dot and Sue found secretarial employment in the city and, during this period, stayed with their grandmother in the suburbs, always keeping close contact with us.

Our time in exile was drawing to a close. We were soon to return to Greystones.

CHAPTER 14

During the 18 months we stayed at Hohenort, we were always aware of Nicky's disability, of our despair and our helplessness. Though he continued to put on weight and grow, there was a distinct deterioration in his appearance. His round, purplish face looked congested and formed a marked contrast to his undeveloped chest and thin knock-kneed legs. He slept badly and often suffered from severe cramp in his legs. A mosquito bite became a swollen supurating sore. He walked with painful slowness. Bill often carried him, or walked with him perched on his shoulder.

He no longer asked me if he would ever be like other boys. He accepted his appearance and his unfitness with pathetic resignation and dignity.

There was so little we could do to help him, except to bolster his courage and not over-protect him.

It was difficult for Bill's gentle and protective nature to deny him anything.

We often had words on the subject.

"Life will be hard enough on him," I said. "But if we spoil him, his life will become unbearable."

He argued. "Give him what happiness we can while he is with us."

We often disagreed on the way to handle our heartbreaking problem, but between us we managed to give him confidence and make him happy. At school, his class, his friends and his teachers continued to build up his morale. Unable to join in boisterous games with other children, he was learning to fall back on his own resources. He read a great deal, and enjoyed adult company; an interested and intelligent listener, at eight he was mature and self-possessed.

We could never completely relax, always haunted with the idea that something might happen to him.

When we returned to Greystones, he showered every morning before going to school. Soon he complained that this hurt his heart. Alarmed, we changed his schedule, and made him bathe at night. He slept deeply each afternoon, re-charging the batteries which kept him going until he went to bed.

The day after we returned to Greystones, Bill, Dirk, and Nicky departed early in the morning to fetch the collie-kelpie which had been sent by train from Nieuwoudtsville. He was three months old; white and gold, with dark-rimmed ravishing brown eyes. We called him Casper. He was cowed and trembling from the ordeal of spending two days and two nights in a wired crate on the train. We were afraid this experience might permanently break his spirit, but after a few days he accepted both us and his new home. He developed a passionate hero worship for Ryk, whom he followed slavishly wherever he went. Unfortunately, Ryk proved to be a wanderer. Every morning when the boys left for school, he waited until Toby and I drove off in the car to do our shopping, then he wandered down the road, staying away for hours.

Once again we were all together at Greystones, though it was only to be for a brief period.

At the end of September, Dot's fiancé arrived from Liberia to stay with us. The whole family, including Anna, awaited his arrival with lively interest. He was short, tough and confident, with fair unruly hair. There was an immediate affinity between him and our two sons, and he met with Anna's full approval.

One day, when we were alone, I said:

"Mervyn, don't you think you should find a job before you marry Dot? When you are settled, she could join you in Rhodesia, or you could come down here and marry her."

He made no reply.

I stole a look at him. He was staring in front of him and his chin was jutting out aggressively.

Three days later, Dot came to me.

"Mom, Mervyn and I want to be married next Wednesday."

There was nothing further we could do. They were married in the morning, and in the evening we gave a small cocktail party for the family and a handful of close friends.

Nicky said to his father, "I want to make a speech."

"No, Nicky. I don't think that's a very good idea."

"Please, Dad!"

Bill lifted him and stood him on the sofa, supporting him with his arm.

"Ladies and gentlemen, Nicky wants to say a few words."

Nicky looked around the room until there was silence, then spoke slowly and clearly.

"Ladies and gentlemen, I want to thank you all for coming to Dot and Mervyn's wedding and for being so kind to them. I think they are very well suited and will be very happy. I want to wish them lots of luck."

73

"Did you prime him?" I asked Bill.

"Not a word. It was entirely his own idea."

The following day we stood on the quay at Cape Town docks waving to them as they leaned from the ship's rail, arms entwined, smiling down at us, about to set out on life's great adventure.

"Au revoir! Bon voyage! Good luck!" we called as the ship slowly moved away.

On returning to Greystones, I found Anna in the dining room, vigorously polishing the table, with tears sliding down her cheeks. She kept her head down, refusing to look at me. Her face was shiny and wet, and she made no effort to wipe the tears away.

"We never see Miss Dot again."

At the end of the year, at Sue's request, Nathan came to spend ten days with us before returning to Israel. We were to find our home treated like a bed-and-breakfast boarding house. They left the house early in the morning, spending the entire day on the beaches of the Peninsula, and coming home in the late evening to change and fly out again. When Nathan returned to Israel, Sue's plans for the future remained indefinite.

We heard regularly from Dot. At first, she was desperately homesick, but soon they had settled in a flat. Mervyn was selling Colliers Encyclopedia and they were starting a family.

Dirk was in the fifth form and in his last year at the preparatory school. During the winter months for the past two years he had played Rugby, fluctuating between the two bottom teams.

Nicky and I watched him run in the Junior School Cross Country Race, on a blisteringly hot day. He came in fifth and walked over to us, hot, sweaty and disgruntled.

"I should have come in fourth. I thought I'd passed the winning post and stopped running. When that other chap ran past me, I realized it was ten yards farther on."

"Why don't you learn to concentrate, Dirk?" I said. "You

must have been the only boy running in that race who didn't know where the winning post was." Utter and complete lack of concentration was his besetting sin.

When we returned home, he called and whistled for the dogs. "Where are Ryk and Casper?" he asked me.

"I don't know. They have probably gone for a walk."

"But they never go for a walk in the afternoon. They are always waiting for me when I come back from school." When they had not returned by nightfall we felt that they had been stolen. The police held out no hope that we would ever see them again. Dirk was heartbroken, and we felt badly.

Six days later, on Sunday morning while we were having tea, Casper ran onto the front lawn barking wildly, deliriously happy to see us. Dirk jumped through the window and clasped him in his arms. He was emaciated, half-starved and covered with thousands of ticks. Young as he was, he had escaped and found his way back to us. After this he never strayed from the house and he and Toby became devoted friends. We never saw Ryk again.

Bill gave Nicky a red bicycle for his eighth birthday.

"It's a ridiculous present," I said. "He will never learn to ride it."

Nor did he. After a few abortive and frightened attempts, he never touched it. Month after month it stood propped up in the garage, gleaming brightly, shiny and new.

CHAPTER 15

I N SEPTEMBER Dot and Mervyn presented us with our first grandchild. She was fair-haired and blue-eyed. They called her Gina. At this time, Sue was going out with an architect who was practicing in Cape Town. Like her, he was tall, good-looking, mercurial and temperamental. Sue called him Ed, but in fact his names were Edmundo Batista Lorenzo Patrick. His father was Italian, his mother Irish and his grandmother French. They were too alike, and frequently had passionate and tempestuous quarrels.

Three months later Dot and Mervyn motored from Rhodesia to spend Christmas with us, and by this time Sue and Ed were engaged: An engagement which was destined to be broken so frequently that Bill and I were in a constant state of bewilderment, never knowing whether the marriage was to take place, or whether they had parted forever.

Dirk was enchanted with his niece; he picked her up and

played with her whenever he found the opportunity. Dot was often indignant to find him sitting on the sofa dandling her on his knee when she should have been asleep. Nicky, less interested, was soon bored with her.

Their brief sojourn with us passed quickly. We were now at the beginning of the new year, 1965.

Dirk was in his first year at college. As usual, Bill, Nicky, and I watched him run at the yearly school Athletics Meeting.

"They told me I must run in the Half-Mile."

"Who is 'they'?"

"The prefect. We had to run different races and he put my name down for the Half-Mile."

Every evening, before the meeting, he and Casper ran down our long road.

"Fletcher should win it, but I think I have a good chance of coming third."

On the day of the meeting it was raining heavily. We parked our car on the Rugby grounds above the field and clambered down the stepped bank, standing huddled under a golf umbrella, close to the track.

Five minutes later, the Half-Mile race started. When they passed us, Dirk was second and Fletcher, the favorite, was third, running easily.

"Dirk has a good, relaxed style," Bill said.

"The trouble about him is, he's too relaxed. I wonder if he's concentrating."

As they finished the first lap, Fletcher slipped in front of him. Dirk was still running third when they passed us with about 220 yards to go. He was relaxed, pink cheeked, breathing easily, running completely within himself.

I could not contain myself.

"Come on Dirk, run!" I shouted.

The effect was dramatic. It could not have been more startling if I had plunged an electric needle into his bottom. He leaped forward and passed Fletcher on the corner; he flashed past the leader, and head up, legs pounding, he streaked down the track, to win the race by twenty yards.

Nicky told Dirk later, "And Mom shouted 'My God, he's going to win!'"

"He's won!" I shouted. "Bill, he's won! Can you believe it?"

Dumbfounded, and pale with shock, Bill was unable to utter a word. Opening his mouth, he shut it again without speaking.

A moment later Dirk loped across the field and stopped wordlessly in front of us, his lips curved in a shy, delighted smile.

At last he had won his cup.

Nicky was pleased with Dirk's success; the boys in his class congratulated him, and he basked contentedly in reflected glory.

A month later a friend telephoned me.

"Mary, there is a friend of mine in Cape Town from England. A well known pediatrician, Dr. Whitney. I've been telling him all about Nicky. He says there is a doctor in London who has done several successful operations on children with Nicky's condition."

There was no quickening of my pulse.

"Are you sure you told him exactly what is wrong with Nicky?"

"I'm almost sure. I believe you are playing tennis with him on Sunday; have a chat with him about it then. He told me he would speak to you."

"I shall most certainly do so. We are showing him the way to the Macdonalds, where we are playing tennis on Sunday afternoon. When we are alone in the car I shall ask him."

When I saw Bill that evening, I told him about our conversation. His reaction like mine was apathetic.

"They've probably got hold of the wrong end of the stick."

Nevertheless, I looked forward to my meeting with Dr. Whitney with immense interest.

He and his wife arrived at Greystones shortly after lunch on Sunday afternoon.

"Let me come with you and show you the way to the tennis courts," I said. "Your wife can go with Bill in our car."

As soon as we were alone, I turned to him.

"I hear that you know about our son Nicky."

"Yes."

"I was also told that you mentioned a surgeon in London who has successfully performed operations on children with the same complaint."

"He has done four, to be exact."

"For what condition?"

"Pulmonary Atresia."

Previously there had been no quickening of my pulse. Now his words caused a physical jolt, and my heart started to pound.

"Were they successful?"

"Three were. The fourth had no hope of survival; the operation in that case was a last desperate attempt to save the child."

"Why hasn't our Cardiac Clinic heard about this? I'm sure they would contact us if they knew there had been successful operations for Pulmonary Atresia."

"This is all very recent and still in the experimental stage. There has not yet been time to write out the full reports of the operations. When this has been done, they will be published, so all cardiac clinics may study them."

"I don't have to tell you what this news means to me: for four years we have virtually been living with a death sentence, always hoping that someday an operation would be found to help him."

"Of course," he said cautiously, "I don't know whether your son would fall into the operative group, but I think it will be well worth your while to write to Angus Charlston and give him a full report."

"We shall do so immediately. Will you give me his address before we part this afternoon?"

80

Bill and I could think and talk of nothing else. The next morning, he telephoned Dr. de Goede, who was as interested as we were, and in a few days he posted a full account of Nicky's condition to Mr. Charlston.

It was several weeks before we received a reply. Time which passed slowly for us, now that the flame of hope was kindled and burning brightly.

"What Dr. Whitney says is perfectly true," Mr. Charlston wrote. "We have operated on a few patients at St. George's and Westminster with a pre-operative diagnosis of Pulmonary Atresia. Most of these have been in the first two years of life. It seems to me that so many cases of so-called Pulmonary Atresia are in reality extreme cases of Fallots Tetralogy, and the only certain way in which to establish the fact that there is a rudimentary outflow tract is by operation. In so many cases angiographic studies tend to be misleading, and it becomes virtually impossible to distinguish between severe tetralogy, which could conceivably be helped, and complete absence of the main pulmonary trunk, which is, from the surgical view, a true atresia.

"Your own studies are so full and so carefully carried out that I would hesitate to suggest any further investigation, but I note he was investigated about four years ago and it is possible one may get some further ciné-angiographic evidence to make the diagnosis absolutely sure.

"We would be happy to see him if you felt it reasonable. After you have carried out the further radiological studies which we suggest, I think it only fair to point out, although we have had our unexpected successes, surgery obviously carries a high risk and it would be unlikely that we could do a complete correction."

There was an enclosed note from Dr. de Goede.

"You will see that it is not as easy as Dr. Whitney made out. We will have to debate whether to do ciné-angio studies on Nicky to see if this better technique can show up the main pulmonary artery or not. You will remember that our two efforts arrived at differentiating between extreme tetralogy and Pulmonary Atresia. The tests appeared to favor the latter: if, of course, he is extreme tetralogy after all, there will be a small pulmonary artery close to the right ventricle.

"The problem is to try and fill a blind sac. We may just succeed with ciné-angio techniques.

"I shall discuss Nicky's problem again at the Cardiac Clinic. Meanwhile, think about it."

"What are ciné-angio studies?" I asked Bill.

"Dr. de Goede wants to do a third catheterization. They have a machine far in advance of the one which was used when Nicky had his last test done. It actually projects moving pictures while the catheterization is being done: this is the ciné-angiographic evidence Mr. Charlston refers to."

"When does he want to do the catheterization?"

His face closed.

"He is discussing the matter at the Cardiac Clinic. There is no hurry."

We were now to endure week and months of uncertainty which was torture for me.

CHAPTER 16

S UE and Ed had a violent culminating quarrel which we assumed had finally disrupted their stormy engagement. She refused to answer the telephone or to see him. "You are too much alike," I said to her. "If you quarrel like this now, it will be ten times worse when you are married. The best thing you can both do is to forget about each other."

To him I said: "Forget about her, Ed. Find yourself a sweet-tempered, placid girl who knows how to handle you."

"But I love her," he said.

A week later, when Toby, the cats, and I were walking in the garden, she joined us.

"Ed and I have been discussing things. We can't go on quarreling like this. We've decided we must get married as soon as possible."

It was the craziest reason I had ever heard of.

"When do you intend getting married?"

"Sometime in August."

"Oh Sue," I wailed. "Can't you make it two months later? It's sure to be pouring with rain. August is a terrible month. We'll never be able to jam 200 people into our small house if it rains."

"We want it to be in August," she repeated firmly.

They were married in August.

"When will you telephone Dr. de Goede and fix the date for Nicky's catheterization?" I asked Bill.

"There's no hurry," he said tersely. "We can discuss it after Sue's wedding."

The first guest arrived at six o'clock. Dirk and Nicky, in long trousers and slicked-down hair, took it upon themselves to greet each guest on the drive as he arrived. Only the first few noticed my flowers; soon our friends and family were standing cheek by jowl, and the noise was deafening. Ed and Sue looked blissfully happy and made a striking couple. The last guest to leave, at half past one, was my brother Helm.

On Monday morning I said to Bill:

"What about phoning Dr. de Goede?"

Immediately his face became strained and tense.

"I'll ring him sometime. There's no hurry."

Six weeks later he left to spend a fishing holiday on the wild coast near Cape Infanta. He kissed me good-by, then paused, his face expressionless.

"I telephoned Dr. de Goede yesterday. He says you may phone him sometime to make an appointment." Another pause. "There's no hurry."

I telephoned at nine o'clock that morning and made an appointment for the beginning of the following week.

That evening when I said goodnight to Nicky, I sat on the edge of his bed and held his hand.

"Nicky, you know that Dad, the doctors, and I have always been looking for something to help you; hoping that some day an operation may be done which would enable you to be like other boys. Next week I'm taking you to Cape Town to see Dr. de Goede. It is now four years since you have seen him. He wants to examine you, and he also wants you to have another catheterization. Can you remember anything about the other two you had?"

He shook his head.

"Not much. I remember it wasn't very nice."

"It won't be very nice this time either. I'm being completely honest with you. I have great respect for your courage."

"Will it be very sore?"

"No. I remember last time you said it wasn't sore, but you will certainly be uncomfortable. I want you to try not to let it upset you. The most important thing to remember is that we are all trying to help you."

He nodded.

"Will I have to go to hospital again?"

"Yes."

"Will Dad be back before I go?"

"Yes."

"When will I go?"

"I don't know. Dr. de Goede will tell us that when he sees us on Tuesday."

On the previous occasion when we had seen Dr. de Goede, he was wan and drawn. Now, when we entered his room, he was relaxed and smiling, greeting us both warmly.

I sat and chatted with him for a few moments. Then he stood up.

"Come on, Nicky, let me have a look at you."

I followed them into the adjoining room and sat on a chair holding Nicky's clothes while he was being examined and X-rayed. An electro-cardiograph was also taken.

When all was done, I dressed him and we returned to the first room.

Dr. de Goede smiled at Nicky.

"Nicky, will you go and read a book in the waiting

room? I want to speak to your mother for a few minutes."

Nicky looked surprised but left without demur.

When we were alone, he turned to me.

"He looks wonderful. Frankly, I am amazed. His heart has not enlarged. He's put on weight, and he has grown."

"Don't you think he's a bit thin?"

"On the contrary, I expected him to be much thinner."

He paused.

"He is, of course, very blue."

"Yes," I said sadly.

"I think he is bluer than he was when I saw him four years ago."

"Yes, I'm sure he is. He seems to have become progressively bluer each year."

"His fingertips too are very heavily clubbed, but his general condition is quite remarkable. I am amazed how he has developed physically."

He looked at me keenly.

"I don't know whether your husband has told you that we are anxious to do another catheterization."

I nodded.

"We now have a machine far in advance of anything we have had before. It actually takes ciné-pictures of the heart. We feel with our present equipment we can do a fuller exploratory examination than we were able to do before. We are hoping to find out a bit more about his pulmonary artery. There is a possibility it may have been completely blocked off since he was last examined. Our main hope is that we find a pulmonary artery which is sufficiently large and near enough to the right ventricle and aorta to permit an operation. With ciné-angio equipment it is possible to shoot a picture without any delay or bother, from any chamber or vessel. With the television screen one sees the dye outlining the particular chamber and vessel injected, and an immediate diagnosis can be made. Later the exposed films can be projected and studied in detail."

"When would you be able to do the catheterization?"

He looked at me inquiringly.

"How soon would you be prepared to have it done?"

"As soon as possible! I can live with anything, except uncertainty."

He nodded sympathetically.

"I can understand that. Would you be prepared to have it done next week?"

"That would be wonderful."

He picked up the telephone and asked his secretary to put him through to Professor Rudolph, the head of the Cardiac Clinic. After a few minutes' conversation, he replaced the receiver.

"It is all arranged. We will do Nicky next Thursday morning. I would like you to take him to Groote Schuur, at two o'clock on Wednesday afternoon, and when you have checked him in to go down with him to the Cardiac Clinic. Professor Rudolph would like to meet you."

As I rose to leave, he said:

"Do you tell him about his condition? Will he know what this is all about?"

"Yes. I tell him everything."

"That is excellent. We find children are much more cooperative if the parents take them into their confidence and tell them what is going to happen. Tell Nicky that this won't be as unpleasant as his last catheterization. It will only take about two hours."

Nicky stood up when we entered the waiting room. He gave me a cheerful smile and shook hands with Dr. de Goede when we left.

As we walked down St. George's Street towards the garage where my car was parked, I took his hand.

"You'll be going to hospital next Wednesday, Nicky."

He looked up at me.

"How long will I be there?"

"Only two days. I'm sorry it's so close to your birthday. We'll have to postpone your party. I'm very sorry about that, but you never know, this may be the most wonderful birthday present you've ever had."

He smiled.

The moment I said it, I regretted it. Bill and I had never accepted the verdict that he was doomed, but we had always been realistic, never building up our hopes with wishful thinking. We knew time was our friend; that yearly, new discoveries were made and new miracles performed. We knew, too, that time was also our enemy: if anything could be found to help him, it must be done before he became too mature.

When Bill returned on Sunday night, he looked tanned and well.

"Nicky's catheterization will be done on Thursday," I said.

His face tightened. Once again the dread, cold hand of fear was upon us.

CHAPTER 17

Nicky approached his third catheterization courage-
ously and with complete acceptance. He knew why
it was being done; he had no illusions that it would be anything
but unpleasant, yet he never once used it as a staff with which
to flay us.

When Bill and I drove him to Groote Schuur Hospital on
Wednesday afternoon, he was talkative and cheerful. Whatever
fears he undoubtedly had, he kept hidden from us. I am convinced this was due to the complete trust he had in us and the
knowledge that we had hidden nothing from him.

Bill dropped us at the front entrance; this time the room
was not so crowded, and I found a place for Nicky at the end
of a bench. I put my bag and coat next to him, so that there
would be a place for me when I rejoined him.

Once again I stood at the window of the office with my
letter from Dr. de Goede. I could not remember if this was the

same man who had spoken to me previously, but the personality was undoubtedly identical: unsmiling, cold, and sour.

Having read the letter and studied a list next to him, he looked up.

"There has been no booking for your son," he said bleakly.

My heart started beating too fast. I knew I should remain calm, but it was beyond me.

"I know—I know a booking has been made," I stammered.

"There is no booking."

I saw Bill at the entrance and beckoned to him agitatedly.

"They say there has been no booking," I said breathlessly.

He could see I was on the verge of tears. He put a steadying hand over mine.

"Go and sit with Nicky. I will speak to him."

Ten minutes later he joined us.

"There was a misunderstanding, but everything is now in order."

He picked up Nicky's suitcase, and we both took his hand and walked to the lift.

The nurse in charge was expecting us when we entered the children's ward, and gave us a friendly greeting.

"Will you take Nicky down to the Cardiac Clinic? Professor Rudolph would like to see you."

We found a bench in the crowded passage next to the door of the Cardiac Clinic. The people sitting on it obligingly made room for us, and we sat down, Nicky perching himself on Bill's knee. The time passed slowly. A constant stream of people moved up and down the passage. An hour later, the door opened and a nurse looked around inquiringly.

"Nicolas Muller?"

We stood up, taking his hand. We entered a small room which was sparsely furnished. There were filing cabinets against the wall and books of files stacked on the high shelves. A tall movable screen hid a medical couch.

Professor Rudolph was sitting behind a large cluttered

desk. He rose, smiling pleasantly, shook hands, and told us to sit down. As I did so, I casually glanced at his desk. A thick dossier lay next to his left hand; across it, in clear printing, was Nicky's name: *Nicolas W. Muller;* and above it "Pulmonary Atresia."

Repeatedly, during his conversation with us, my eyes returned to it with fascinated horror. He examined Nicky briefly, and once again sat down behind his desk, facing us.

"I believe Dr. de Goede has explained to you the ciné-angio machine we have been using for the last two years. We feel this should enable us to discover more about Nicky's pulmonary artery. Would you like to see it?" he asked Nicky.

Nicky nodded.

Professor Rudolph took us into the adjoining room and introduced us to a white-coated doctor.

"This is Dr. Allen. He and Dr. de Goede will be doing the catheterization tomorrow. He will show you how the machine works."

I looked at the narrow couch on which Nicky would be lying the next morning and wondered what his feelings were. I stole a look at him, but his face was expressionless.

We followed Dr. Allen into a small room on the left obviously used for storing files and records. On the shelves were row upon row of round metal containers. He took one down, looked at it, and replaced it. He studied several tins, and finally found what he was looking for.

"This is the film of a four-year-old Indian boy with Pulmonary Atresia."

We watched with fascinated interest as he opened the container and removed the film.

The curtains were drawn, the light switched off, and on a television screen next to the couch we saw the catheter slowly enter the heart chamber, and the small explosion of dye as it did so. The next day, Nicky would lie on his side on the couch and see the identical picture, knowing then that it would be his own heart he was watching.

When we returned to the children's ward, a nurse showed us his bed, quickly undressed him and put on his pajamas. We stayed with him until six o'clock. We kissed him good-by and he smiled at us, but his tremulous mouth betrayed him. When we stopped at the door and looked back he was staring steadfastly out of the window.

Once again we sat in silence that night, unable to refer to our mutual misgivings.

I arrived at the children's ward punctually at two o'clock. Nicky was lying on his side, with a book over his face. My heart sank.

"He's crying," I thought.

However, he looked up and smiled and I saw no trace of tears, or any sign of the drained exhaustion I had witnessed previously.

"Was it very horrible?" I asked.

"No. It wasn't so bad. There was some stuff they injected into my arm that burned like hell, but whenever they did it, Dr. de Goede gave me orange juice to drink. He's very nice, you know. He told me I'm the best patient he's ever had."

"I knew you'd be brave. I'm very proud of you."

When I returned to Greystones, I changed into a pair of slacks and wandered aimlessly around the garden trying to discipline my feverish mind. October is a beautiful month in the Cape. The herbaceous border was planted out and full of promise; the roses were in their first flush, and the garden was sweet with the scent of woodbine.

I was crouched under the old wild laurel picking primroses when Anna walked around the corner of the house and called me.

"Is tea ready?" I asked.

"Na. The doctor wants to speak to Madam on the phone."

My heart lurched and started to beat quickly. It could only

be good news! He had never telephoned me before. Wild, unreasoning hope surged up in an uncontrollable wave.

I forced myself to walk slowly.

I sat down, picked up the receiver, and took a deep breath. "Hello."

"Hello. Hello. Hello."

The exuberance and gaiety of his voice raised my hopes to such a pitch that I felt a sensation of suffocation.

"We worked on Nicky for two hours this morning. We started on the right side of his heart first and after an hour found everything we had found before. We then started on the left side. I was able to pass the tip of the catheter through a hole in the wall between the two atria. Once in the left atrium it was simple to reach the left ventricle and it was absolute drama: we could not believe our eyes. An angiogram from this site revealed a large pulmonary artery coming off the left ventricle, and we at once realized that the diagnosis was Transposition of the Great Vessels and not Pulmonary Atresia."

"Is it operable?" I interrupted.

"Yes. This operation has been performed with brilliant success at the Mayo Clinic for the last four years."

"Oh! How wonderful!"

"Yes. Isn't it wonderful."

"What actually is wrong with his heart?"

"In this condition the pulmonary artery comes off the left ventricle and the aorta from the right ventricle. This is the complete opposite of the normal situation. The result is that the right ventricle ejects blue blood into the aorta, resulting in severe cyanosis—that is, blueness; and the left ventricle pumps red blood back into the lungs. If there is no communication or hole between the two circulations, death occurs very soon after birth. Children born with Transposition of the Great Vessels seldom survive—it is a miracle that Nicky is alive."

"I still can't believe it."

"Yes. It is unbelievable. We are all highly delighted. Professor Rudolph would like to see you and your husband tomorrow morning when you fetch Nicky. I will meet you in the children's ward and take you down to the Cardiac Clinic."

"Thank you for phoning me."

"I felt I had to let you know as soon as possible."

"Thank you."

I put the receiver down and burst into tears.

CHAPTER 18

DIRK insisted on driving to Groote Schuur Hospital with us the next morning. "But you won't be allowed in the children's ward," I said.

"I know," Dirk replied. "I'll wait in the car."

"You may have to wait for a long time. We have to go down to the Cardiac Clinic and may be there for over an hour."

"I don't mind."

Bill dropped me at the entrance, and I walked up to the children's ward ahead of him. Nicky was sitting in bed watching the door and was delighted to see me.

I kissed him.

"Come on. Stand up and I'll dress you. Dr. de Goede will be here soon."

"Where's Dad?"

"He'll be here in a minute."

He was standing on the bed, half-dressed, holding onto my shoulder, when Bill entered the ward.

"Have you told him?" he asked me.

"No, I was waiting for you."

He kissed Nicky and held his hand.

"Nicky, they have found they can operate on you and make you better. One day you will be just like other boys."

He gave a single soft cry of pleasure and burst into laughter. He jumped up and down on the bed, clinging onto Bill's hand and my shoulder, wordlessly expressing his delight.

Dr. de Goede entered the ward a few minutes later, and we shook hands with impulsive warmth.

"The problem with Pulmonary Atresia," he said, "is that the pulmonary artery does not fill with radio-opaque dye when this is injected into the right ventricle or aorta. If one can't visualize it, one cannot say if an operation will be possible. The fact that Dr. Charlston had something to offer made it essential to try again, to save you a fruitless and perhaps disastrous operation. With ciné-angiographic methods I thought we might just see some dye pouring from the aorta into the pulmonary artery."

He smiled.

"I was also very thrilled to get another chance to study Nicky, now that we had new equipment, because I had never been completely convinced that he was a case of Pulmonary Atresia. He should have had loud continuous murmurs over his chest, which are almost invariable with patients who survive this condition.

"Nicky, who was doing so well, never had these signs, and this always worried me. So when the chance came to re-catheterize, we made quite sure to shoot pictures from all chambers, especially the left side of the heart.

"This gave the diagnosis. Previously, we had not been able to enter the left ventricle and had a rather fixed object of differentiating between Fallots Tetralogy and Pulmonary Atresia."

"I don't think I have to tell you what this news means to us," Bill said, his voice charged with emotion.

I remembered the last time we had seen Dr. de Goede in this same room. How strained and haggard he had looked; how our faces, too, must have reflected our agony. Now, joy and happiness radiated from all of us.

We left the children's ward and walked down to the Cardiac Clinic, which was at the far end of the hospital. Professor Rudolph and Dr. Allen seemed pleased to see us.

"We are all absolutely delighted," said Professor Rudolph. "We unhesitatingly admit that the original diagnosis was completely incorrect."

"What a wonderful admission," I interrupted.

Dr. de Goede laughed.

Professor Rudolph looked at him with a smile.

"He would never give in," he told us. "He was not happy about the diagnosis, and he never allowed us to forget about Nicky. At meeting after meeting, he brought his name up."

He paused.

"As Dr. de Goede told you, Nicky had complete Transposition of the Great Vessels, which is a rare heart condition which has been successfully operated on in the United States for the last four years."

"Have they done this operation in Cape Town?"

He paused. "One was performed in an endeavor to save the child's life. It was not successful.

"Our advice to you is to take him to the Mayo Clinic at Rochester in the United States, where Doctor Abbot, a world famous cardiac surgeon, has specialized in this particular operation and performed it with great success over the last four years."

"How successful is the operation?"

"Complete normality."

The words caused almost a physical shock. Never had we dared hope for such an incredible miracle.

"Nicky!" I cried, ruffling his hair.

He looked up and smiled at me.

"It will of course be extremely expensive," said Professor Rudolph, looking at Bill. "I don't know whether you feel you can afford to do this."

"Please don't consider the financial side of it," Bill said. "I'll find the money somehow. We will naturally want him to go to the place where he will have the best chance. How do we set about it?"

"I know Dr. Abbot and will write to him personally to fix a date for the operation. As soon as we have a reply from him, we shall let you know. You will be taking him to the best place in the world for this particular operation."

We shook hands with the three men who in one brief moment had removed the sword of Damocles poised above us all these years.

I had forgotten about Dirk, who was still sitting in the back of the car. He opened the door for Nicky and, as he climbed in, put his arms around him and kissed him.

We drove straight to my mother-in-law's home to share our wonderful news, knowing how much it would mean to her. For ten years she had shared our heavy burden, a strain not lightly borne by a woman of nearly 87 years.

She immediately said: "As you know, I have put money aside for Nicky's operation. It is there whenever you need it."

Her faith in his ultimate survival had never flagged.

"I will also help you," Aunt Etta said.

These were the first two hands spontaneously held out to help us. There were to be many more.

During the bad years Bill and I had become increasingly aware that we had wonderful friends. We were ever conscious of their sympathy, their kindness and affection. Now, when the sun broke through the dark clouds shadowing our lives, their sharing in our joy was deeply touching, and hands were impulsively held out to help ease our financial burden.

Letters arrived.

"It would give me a very great happiness to feel I was contributing just a little bit towards giving him a chance of the fine healthy future to which such a splendid brave boy is entitled."

Another wrote: "Will you please accept this in the spirit in which it is meant. It's the life of a little child. I don't think it is necessary to say any more."

We were to experience kindness and generosity beyond belief; to be swept up in an embracing wave of goodwill and affection which strengthened our courage for the ordeal which lay ahead.

I wrote a letter to Dr. de Goede thanking him for all he had done for us. He replied a few days later.

"All this goes to show what a great responsibility it is carrying out these diagnostic tests, and what an enormous help it is to have all the modern equipment and such good technical assistance. Fortunately, the delay in the diagnosis has been to Nicky's advantage, because it is only in the last six months or so that we have begun to feel really confident about the surgical results in the clever operation devised for this condition.

"As you rightly say, now that we know, the sooner the better, and I shall let you know the moment Professor Rudolph has heard from Dr. Abbot."

To our family doctor he wrote:

"Dr. Abbot of the Mayo Clinic has had very good results with this operation in this type of transposition.

"I need hardly mention how delighted we all feel with the diagnosis and the prospect that something really effective can be done for this highly intelligent and courageous youngster."

"How long do you think it will take before we hear from them?" I asked Bill.

"It will probably take about a month."

We discussed from every angle who should be the one to take Nicky over to the United States. While he had always been more demonstrative in his love for his father, we both recognized that I was better able to build up his courage and self-respect and could handle him better in emotional stress. This Nicky himself recognized. There was no doubt that I must be the one to take him.

Six weeks passed and we heard no word from Dr. Abbot. Weeks which passed agonizingly slowly for us. Now our family doctor, Nicky's godfather, actively intervened.

"I have a young friend named Dr. Joubert who comes from Cape Town. He has been a fellow at Mayo Clinic for the last 18 months, and for a while he was Dr. Abbot's second assistant. I've written and asked him to find out why we have not yet received a reply from the Mayo Clinic. I think it would also be a good idea for Bill to write to him and send the full catheterization report for them to study."

Bill did so immediately, and a fortnight later received a letter from Dr. Abbot.

"Dr. Joubert has turned over to me your letter of the twelfth of November. I am terribly sorry for the delay in answering the letter from Professor Rudolph.

"I in fact did get Professor Rudolph's letter and have just recently written to him. I agree one hundred percent with Professor Rudolph that your boy is a very good candidate for surgery. By this I mean, he should have at least nine chances out of ten, and probably more, of surviving. Furthermore, his long-term result should be excellent.

"Thus, I think there is much hope for his future. We are corresponding with Professor Rudolph and will be arranging the details of his coming visit."

We sent copies of this letter to our friends, so that they could fully participate in the adventure in which they were playing so large a part.

Weeks passed, and we heard nothing further. Once again Nicky's godfather set things in motion.

"As you know, Dr. Thomas, who examined Nicky eight years ago, was at the Mayo Clinic for many years. He is well remembered there, and I'm sure he'll be able to help you.

Come around tomorrow evening and have a talk with him."

When I met him, he spoke glowingly of Dr. Abbot's immense ability.

"Now tell me exactly how you set about things to arrange this operation. This sounds unlike the Mayo Clinic that is highly efficient and prompt. What was the first thing that you did?"

"Professor Rudolph wrote a personal letter to Dr. Abbot and—"

"Wrong from the start!" he interrupted loudly. "It should have been done from the bottom, through the usual channels. Dr. Abbot obviously assumes this has been done. He would expect them to bring up the matter with him and discuss it. Give me a piece of paper, and I'll write a letter."

Three weeks later, on the tenth of January, Bill received the following letter from Dr. Abbot:

"As I am sure you must know, there is a tremendous demand for this type of surgery, and because of it our operative schedule is rather crowded for many months ahead. Actually, it is only by virtue of a cancellation that I am able to offer your son the surgical date of the fifteenth of April. I am most regretful that it is so far off. I do hope, however, that you can see your way clear to accepting this date.

"If so, we would like your boy to report to the Mayo Clinic on the seventh of April, 1966."

CHAPTER 19

THE bad years were over. I wrote to my old school friend Anni Fincham, whose husband was the South African Consul General in New York, to tell her our news about Nicky. She immediately invited us to spend a week with them in New York, and I accepted this invitation with great pleasure.

We were concerned about Nicky's entry into the United States, since he had not been vaccinated.

His godfather gave us the following medical certificate:

"This is to certify that owing to a serious heart complaint from birth, it is medically inadvisable for Nicolas Muller to be vaccinated. He is booked to go to America for an open heart operation."

Bill took the further precaution of writing to the Department of Health, Staten Island, New York.

They replied: "Have your son carry with him and present

to the Public Health inspector at New York, the statements of your doctor and the Health Department, copies of which documents you sent me in your letter. Health inspectors at Kennedy International Airport, New York, will be notified in advance of his arrival of the special problem. Carrying the documents with him will assist identification and help expedite clearance.

"Vaccination will not be required because of medical contraindication by your doctor."

I wrote to Dr. Joubert, the young South African doctor at the Mayo Clinic, asking him if he could arrange accommodations for us in Rochester. I was taken aback at his suggestion that we should stay in a motel close to Saint Mary's Hospital.

"It has a double bedroom, a fully stocked kitchenette, and a large sitting room."

"A motel!" I said to Bill. "I'll have to cook, make the beds, and wash up!"

But the more I thought of it, the better I liked the idea. We would be completely independent, and it would keep me occupied.

He added, at the end of his letter:

"Let me know when your plane is due to arrive in Rochester, and my wife and I will meet you at the airport."

I said to Bill: "Anni will meet us in New York, the Jouberts in Rochester. The place I'm worrying about is Chicago; we have to change planes there for our flight to Rochester and I'm so frightened that I'll do something stupid and miss the connection."

"An agent will meet you there and assist you."

"But say he's not there!"

He smiled indulgently.

"Stop worrying: of course he'll be there. Everything has been arranged."

We were booked to fly from Cape Town to Jan Smuts, Johannesburg, on the twenty-ninth of March, and leave the following day for the United States.

Spiritually and mentally I was already on the wing. Every nerve and thought was focused on the future. It was apparent that Nicky too could think of little else. Every morning he came into my room in his dressing gown, sat on his father's bed and smiled at me.

"We'll be leaving in 50 days."

Or—

"We'll be leaving in 45 days."

"Forty-one days left!"

Dr. Thomas lent me a medical journal containing an excellent article by a doctor from Cape Town who had taken his son to Rochester for cardiac surgery by Dr. Abbot. It gave a graphic description of the patient after the operation: he would be naked, ice cold, with tubes coming from his body and an oxygen mask over his face: the article emphasized how important it was to tell the child all this before the operation took place, so he would know what to expect.

I read the article to Nicky, explaining in detail anything he did not understand.

"You see, Nicky, they say it is most important that you should know everything. They say too that I must come and see you once an hour, so that you will know I am always near you."

Dr. Helen Frazer, who had met her husband at the Mayo Clinic, told me about Rochester, the Clinic, and Saint Mary's Hospital.

"I'm thinking of going to the States soon. There is a possibility I may be in Rochester when you are there."

She gave me an article on cardiac surgery and a booklet on Rochester. These, too, I shared with Nicky. I often discussed his operation with him, and any new information I gleaned I immediately imparted to him.

I always referred to our trip as The Great Adventure.

It was a time of strain, excitement, and preparation. Our outlook on life was completely changed. The tension was still there, but now we looked to the future with immense hope. Often Nicky appeared blue, tired, and pathetic, but it was no longer a dagger in our hearts.

"How different he will look in three months," we thought.

In February Dot presented us with our second grandchild. Another daughter, whom they called Collette.

Ever since Dirk had had his small success in the Half Mile, he had been fired with ambition.

For months he and Casper ran every evening; sometimes around the gracious homes of Bishopscourt Estate, or up the mountain and along the contour path. Often he ran up the hill to the Hen and Chickens Estate and through the beautiful Kirstenbosch gardens.

"There are hundreds of sugarbirds sipping honey from the proteas. Not dozens. Hundreds. I stopped to look at them. Some are bright burnished green and others have tails about fifteen inches long with bright green and red breasts. You should go and see them—they're beautiful."

Often he burst into my room in the morning.

"Look out of the window. There are six guinea-fowl on the lawn."

Three weeks before the annual Athletic Meeting, Dirk stayed on at school every afternoon to have intensive training by a master who had himself represented South Africa in the Mile and Half-Mile events.

"I ran eight quarter-miles today," he said.

"Surely that can't be good for him!" I said to Bill.

The next day he grinned and said:

"Today I ran four half-miles."

"Bill, I'm sure this is too strenuous. He only turned 14 three months ago. Aren't you tired, Dirk?"

"No. I feel fine."

On the day of the meet, Bill was away on a fishing holiday, deeply disappointed to miss Dirk's races in which he had taken such an active interest.

It was a beautiful day. The sky was blue and clear, the sun was shining brightly and there was a pleasant cool southeasterly breeze. Nicky and two of my friends accompanied me. As soon as we reached the field, Nicky left us and joined a group of his friends, who greeted him noisily.

We found a cool place, close to the track, under a small group of pine trees. We were soon joined by Sue, and Nicky's godfather. Dirk sat on the grassy bank behind us. He was very quiet. Half an hour before his race he left us and walked aimlessly across the field, looking very young and slender in his navy track suit.

Five minutes before the Half-Mile race we were joined by Nicky and a large contingent of small boys who stood in a solid group immediately behind us.

We watched them line up. Behind them the white-coated starter pointed his pistol to the sky. We saw the small white puff of smoke before we heard the actual report.

When they passed us Dirk was running first, with Fletcher once again breathing down his neck. Dirk was running strongly. His jaw was jutting out and his face was grimly determined.

"Good Lord," I whispered in awe. "He's concentrating."

"Come on, Dirk! Come on, Muller!" Nicky and his friends shouted in piping trebles.

When they passed us in the second lap, Fletcher and Dirk were well ahead of the rest of the field, but now Fletcher's mouth was open and his knees were rising high. Dirk pulled away from him and won his race with ease.

Once again he loped across the field to join us, with two small admirers at his heels. Nicky walked up to him and shook his hand.

In the afternoon he won the Under Fifteen Mile and broke the school record.

The next day Dr. Helen Frazer telephoned me.

"I'm leaving for the States tomorrow; I've phoned to say good-by. When is Nicky's operation taking place?"

"On the fifteenth of April."

A pause.

"I may be in Rochester then."

During these months of waiting I was unable to sleep and became tense and brittle. My sense of humor flagged. Every nerve strained to be on our way.

Slowly and inexorably our time of departure drew near.

Friends rallied around us. In a hundred different ways they demonstrated their affection and concern. Never were two people more warmly encouraged.

Bill's sister Marjorie suggested that on our flight to the United States, Nicky and I should break our journey and spend the night with them in Pretoria.

We booked to fly from the D. F. Malan Airport on Wednesday the twenty-ninth of March.

I gave a farewell dinner at Greystones to which I invited members of Bill's family and mine.

"Nicky," I said. "I want you to make a speech tonight."

He took this request extremely seriously. Later I found scribbled notes of his speech lying on my dressing table.

"Ladies and gentlemen," he said. "I want to thank you all for coming here tonight and bidding me farewell before my trip to the United States. I also want to thank you for how kind you've been to all of us.

"This operation will be the most wonderful thing that has ever happened to me.

"When I get back, you must all come to the airport to meet me."

The last remark was met with a loud burst of laughter from the family.

Disconcerted, he abruptly sat down, bending his head to hide his shy smile.

THE
GREAT
ADVENTURE

Part II

CHAPTER 1

THE day had arrived. I awoke early on that cold clear morning, put on my dressing gown, and stood at the window looking across the valley. Thin wisps of mist were slowly spiraling and evaporating in the early morning sun. The herringbones of the vineyards were clearly etched, and the row of serried pines stood out starkly: the only formal touch in that gracious and rural valley. In the far distance, the pale grey mist still clung to the wooded flanks of Constantiaberg.

I had one of those moments of self-dramatization which we all indulge in at some period in our lives. How would I feel the next time I stood at this window and looked down on the valley I loved so dearly? Would it be with joy and humble gratitude? Would it be without the sorrow and pain which had been with me all these years, like a cancer gnawing at my very soul? Or would it be with deep sadness and bleak desolation?

So many conflicting emotions were swirling and twisting

in my mind. Fear, hope, determination, and sheer misery. Pressing me down with its frightening weight was the awful responsibility resting on my shoulders; the decisions I would be called upon to make. The impending loneliness.

I knew I must be Nicky's bulwark and strength, his anchor and his gay-love; I must give him gaiety and companionship.

The previous night I had sat up late writing to say farewell to the friends who had supported and helped us in so many different ways during the past few weeks.

"When you read this, Nicky and I will be on the wing, setting out on the greatest adventure of both our lives. We go, I know, with the affection and good wishes of all our friends. This is just a note to say 'Tot siens' and to bring you our love."

The four of us spent that morning in close communion. By mutual consent, the trip was never mentioned. I walked around the garden with the two dogs at my heels, the cats accompanying us in erratic spurts and dashes. Even now, on this last day, I walked with the snippers in my hand, pausing to cut out a piece of dead wood or a dead flower, forcing my mind to remain blank and passive.

I sat in the spare room and wrote a letter to Bill.

"When you read this, Nicky and I will be on our way, and you and Dirk alone together at Greystones. I am sure you will find Dirk a great comfort and will miss him very much when he leaves you for the Easter weekend.

"I want to apologize for being so horrid to you the last few months. I know that you recognized this for a build-up of tension. I still can't think why it should have the effect of making me nasty to the person I love most in the world. The psychologists could probably explain.

"This is to say 'Tot siens.'

"I shall miss your strength and companionship very much."

Dirk walked out of the house and sat next to me.

"Mom, I think Nicky is crying. He is standing by himself

in the spare room, staring down the valley, and when I walked in, he was wiping his eyes."

I quickly went upstairs.

He was standing at the window. He gave me a quick look and turned his face away, but not before I saw his reddened eyes.

"Nicky, come and help me pack," I said casually.

He followed me obediently, sitting on his father's bed while I put the last few things into our suitcases.

"Nicky," I said, "with going away, there is fun and excitement and there is also sadness. At this moment, like you, I too feel sad."

His lip quivered. This poignant, tremulous movement of his mouth caused the tears to well into my eyes, and in a moment they had spilled over and were flowing down my cheeks. When he saw this, he too began to cry. This spontaneous sharing of tears welded us together as nothing else could have done. In this secret moment, a companionship and closeness was born.

I sat down and dried my eyes, shaking my head.

"This is terrible. Think how ridiculous we must look. Imagine how awful it would be if one of the family walked in and found the two of us sitting here, crying."

He gave a snort of laughter. This ridiculous sound made us giggle, and then laugh wildly, with a touch of hysteria. I stood up and ran cold water into the basin. I washed his face and my own, then powdered my nose. There was one further thing I must say to him.

"Nicky, whatever happens, you and I must not cry at the airport. If we break down it will be harrowing and embarrassing for the friends and family who have come to see us. When we are in the plane, we may cry as much as we like."

He now looked at me levelly, not attempting to hide his tear-stained eyes, and nodded.

Nicky was very brave at the airport.

When we entered the plane, he sat for a while with his back to me, and I left him in peace. Later, he dried his eyes and was interested to see the Orange River. Its banks were the only green in the brown, arid map below us. Before touching down at Kimberley, he saw the Big Hole, the great original diamond mine, now half-filled with brown water.

The flight from Kimberley to the Jan Smuts Airport in Johannesburg was brief and pleasant; as we walked across the tarmac towards the Airport I squeezed his hand.

"Look! There's Marjorie and the children to meet us."

They stood in the doorway, smiling and waving at us.

Nicky was silent and unresponsive during the drive to Pretoria, but once we reached Marjorie's house I was pleased to hear him talking and laughing with the other children. Before dinner Bill telephoned from Cape Town and we spoke to the family, but I was so strained and emotional that speaking to them was difficult. Nicky had a long conversation with Dirk and returned to the room laughing loudly.

"Dirk says, when our plane flew off, Anna wailed 'Ooh-la! Ooo-la!' "

I smiled and whispered to myself, "We never see Madam and Nicky again."

Friends telephoned from Johannesburg and Pretoria to wish us Godspeed and good luck.

As I replaced the receiver, Nicky walked into the room and sat down on the arm of my chair, placing his hand on my shoulder.

"I've just thrown up," he whispered.

"Where?" I asked apprehensively.

"Outside, in a bush."

He was tired and overwrought. Shortly after dinner I put him to bed.

The next day we boarded the plane at Jan Smuts at quarter to three.

Nicky was drawn and blue. We were to endure a marathon flight across the African Continent and over the Atlantic to New York.

We arrived at Leopoldville in the evening. It was hot and humid, as we had expected, but the air was not oppressive. We walked across the tarmac to the airport to find something cool to drink. Walking with Nicky was always a painful and tortuous process; his pace was slow, with frequent pauses to regain his breath.

On the way to Lagos, darkness fell. This was the beginning of an interminable 18-hour night. We stopped at Accra, Robertsville and finally Dakar. I looked out of the window and saw the first lights of Dakar; as we swooped down I saw their brilliance reflected like jewels in the sea.

The pilot made a perfect landing. I woke Nicky and put on his jersey. We stepped into the night. It was cool. There was the fresh, salty tang of the sea. We breathed in hungrily, filling our lungs with the clean, sweet air.

At the airport we washed our faces and brushed our teeth. We freshened and fortified ourselves for the eight-hour night flight across the Atlantic, which lay before us.

In South African time, it was now five o'clock in the morning. In American time, it was ten o'clock at night.

By the time the first pale honeyed light of dawn appeared on the horizon, Nicky and I had been awake for some time. We were both hungry. It was 16 hours since our dinner, before touching down at Lagos, and we were now famished. He disinterestedly nibbled a piece of chocolate. Two hours later we ravenously fell upon our breakfast.

An hour later, at half past eight on a raw grey morning, we arrived at the John Kennedy Airport in New York. As we walked wearily towards the Airport, I glanced up and saw Anni waving to us from the balcony. A warm flood of relief flowed over me. Here was an old friend to meet us in this great, strange land. Here was somebody who for a moment could ease the heavy burden weighing me down.

Nicky was very tired. On the way through Immigration and the Customs, he squatted on his haunches next to the little bag he was carrying, blue and heavy-eyed, pathetically resigned to his discomforts, as he had been throughout this exhausting trip.

There was no hitch with the Health authorities. They read the two letters I handed them with interest, took one look at Nicky's drained, blue face and waved us through. In a few moments Anni was welcoming us to New York.

What luxury to sit in the back of the car with Anni and Nicky; to stretch out my cramped legs and know we had at last arrived. Nicky, still heavy-eyed, was now alert and eagerly gazing out of the window.

Nicky and I fell in love with New York on sight.

Anni and Charles lived in an apartment in Park Avenue. The awning at the entrance was typical of that area of New York. A door man darted out and opened the door of our car. We entered a graciously furnished foyer and an elevatorman took us up to the first floor. We walked into the apartment which was to be our home for the next week.

Charles was there, waiting to give us a warm and affectionate welcome. A sumptuous breakfast was prepared for us, to which we were unable to do justice.

Nicky's immediate request was to see television. Within a few minutes he was sitting perched on the edge of his chair, staring in mesmerized fascination.

Anni took me into the charming and luxurious bedroom Nicky and I were to share. I quickly unpacked our things and then relaxed in a hot bath, feeling the tiredness and strain slowly draining out of me. An hour later, I took a loudly protesting Nicky from the television set and put him to bed. He immediately fell asleep and awoke nine hours later.

We were to spend a stimulating and exciting week in New York. Anni and Charles were determined to show us as much of this fascinating city as possible in the short time we were with them. Nicky proved an entrancing and intensely interested companion. I think we both consciously put all thought of the future from our minds and lived entirely in the excitement and glamor of the present.

We naturally went up to the top of the Empire State Building, but this paled in comparison to the breathtaking view from the dining room at the top of Chase-Manhattan in Wall Street, where we looked down on the broad expanse of the Hudson River. It was from there we saw the green Statue of Liberty, so much smaller than I had imagined her to be. From another window we looked uptown to the cluster of immense skyscrapers, dominated by the Empire State Building and the slender silver spire of the Chrysler Building gleaming brightly in the sun.

I took him to the Metropolitan Museum and introduced him to the Impressionists: Renoir's opulent peaches in the blue and white dish; Van Gogh's inscrutable and sinister looking mother.

Nicky disappeared at regular intervals to buy himself a hot dog. He had developed a consuming passion for frankfurters.

We saw the Rockefeller Center at night with Nicky perched on Charles' shoulder and stood watching a group of young people skating on the ice below us.

We walked up glittering, colorful, vulgar Broadway, jostled by its teeming mass of people, and saw men sleeping on the sidewalks of The Bowery.

We rubbed shoulders with the beatniks and bohemians of Greenwich Village, and walked the quiet streets of Chinatown among the most law-abiding citizens of New York.

We were bewildered by the dense, fast-moving traffic and the thousands of taxis.

We drove through the immense Central Park, with its many beautiful trees and its strange outcrops of rock, so typical of Manhattan.

All the time we were in New York it was bitterly cold; spring was late and the trees were still stark and leafless. We found it difficult to accustom ourselves to the intense cold outside and the unbearably overheated stuffiness of the stores and apartments.

The stores were immense and bewildering. Marbled floors. Departments flowing into each other. So many people and so much displayed that I was stupefied.

And suddenly the New York interlude was over.

I was packing our bags and the tension was back. The excitement had died from Nicky's eyes and he was silent.

They drove us to the John Kennedy Airport.

A clasp around the shoulders from Anni.

"Remember we are always here if you should need us. Don't hesitate to phone if we can help you: after all, we are only a few hours apart."

CHAPTER 2

IT WAS a lovely day. Our flight to Chicago was pleasant and uneventful. Nicky was flattered to find a small packet of cigarettes on his lunch tray. He also received a junior-pilot badge, which he pinned onto his jersey below the well earned one he had got on our marathon flight to New York.

Twenty minutes before we landed, we flew over an immense grey lake of turbulent water, stretching as far as the eye could see, until in the far distance we saw the softly blurred skyscrapers of Chicago. We flew inland and five minutes later touched down with a perfect landing.

As we entered the airport I tensely scanned the waiting crowd. There was no one to meet us. At the door, I saw a cluster of small trolleys and took one for my coats and bags. We followed the crowd down a long wide passage. Nicky tired quickly. His face was bluish-grey and his breathing distressed. He stopped. "My heart is sore."

My own heart began to beat wildly. I gathered him in my arms and put his feet on the edge of the trolley.

"Put your hands on the rail and hold tight."

I pushed him down one passage after another, muttering prayers of thanks that I had some means of conveyance for him, as the distance was far beyond anything he could possibly have endured.

We now came to a staircase with a notice saying that no trolleys could be taken beyond this point. My heart sank. I helped him off the trolley, took my coats and bags, and followed him down the escalator.

Here we found the counter where we could collect our baggage. I gave my tickets to an elderly porter who quickly collected our two suitcases and placed them on a large trolley.

Walking slowly down the wide corridor, he told us to follow him.

I called him to stop.

"Please put my son on top of the suitcases. He cannot walk any farther."

With fatherly solicitude and an expression of intense concern, he lifted Nicky and put him on top of our baggage. We moved on slowly, once more traversing one interminable passage after another.

We ultimately arrived at the Northwestern Airlines Terminal.

Our porter said he would now have to leave us.

"Sit down and relax, Madam. Your flight is not due for another 45 minutes. I shall ask my friend to bring you a wheel-chair for your son for the final walk."

A few minutes later he returned, accompanied by another porter who promptly found a wheelchair. He showed us where to put it, assuring us that he would inform us as soon as our flight was called.

We found a sofa near the window and I sat down, sinking back wearily. I opened my cigarette case, took out a cigarette and lit it, not surprised to find my hand was trembling.

We sat in silence for a long while. Nicky slowly relaxed, and his face lost the tense, strained expression which had frightened me so much.

"Is your heart still hurting you?"

"No, it feels better now. I wonder why nobody met us."

"I don't know, but everything is going to be all right now. I was so worried we might miss the plane to Rochester."

"What would you have done if we had?" he asked, smiling.

"I'd rather not even think about it," I said, with an expressive shudder.

Half an hour later our porter appeared and assisted Nicky into the wheelchair. We leisurely made our way to the final room. It was with relief that I settled Nicky into the seat next to the window and fastened the buckle of my seat belt. The flight to Rochester was short, with one stop on the way.

Looking down, I could see the country was farmland with densely wooded hills. Some of the fields were plowed, and the soil was richly brown. Drifts of snow still lay in the hollows and in the ditches next to the winding roads. Here and there we saw a farm house, the dwelling dwarfed by the great hip-roofed barn. Many of the houses and barns were a glowing burgundy red. The trees were bare and silvery grey. It was obvious that winter had not yet released her grip.

When we stepped out of the plane, Nicky was excited to see a pile of snow shoveled against the side of a barn. He wanted to go across and touch it, to feel what snow was like. Impatiently I made him stay near me, once again anxiously scanning the crowd.

A woman's voice said:

"Excuse me. Are you Mrs. Muller?"

I found myself looking at a pretty fair-haired girl. Her resemblance to Dot was startling.

"Yes. Are you Mrs. Joubert?"

"I didn't think it could be you. Your son is dressed like

an American. I didn't expect to see him wearing an anorak."

A moment later her husband joined us. He had a crewcut. His lean, intelligent face at the moment was tense and strained.

"We thought you had missed the plane. We came to meet you yesterday. What happened?"

"But we were only supposed to arrive today."

"No. You were due to arrive yesterday. Nicky's first appointment at the Clinic was at nine o'clock this morning. They were rather upset he wasn't there."

"I'm sure you are wrong," I said.

I opened my bag and took out my engagement book. He was correct. We had arrived a day late.

"I can't believe it. I can't tell you how sorry I am this has happened. The booking was incorrect from the start. It is hard to imagine how we failed to notice it."

Seeing my consternation, he thawed and forgave me. He took my baggage ticket, collected our luggage, and a moment later we all clambered into their Volkswagen.

On the drive to Rochester he stopped the car next to a drift of snow lying in a hollow by the roadside. He and Nicky got out and walked in it. Nicky touched it, ate it, made a big snowball, and threw it at the car. His little face, blue as ever, was shining with excitement.

It was a heart-warming little episode, and one of many instances of the kindness and thoughtfulness we would experience from this young couple.

We entered the town and drove up a wide avenue. Peter Joubert turned the car sharply and stopped in front of two small, square three-storied buildings.

"This is your motel. And there," pointing to the right on the opposite side of the road, "is Saint Mary's Hospital." It was an immensely long, gracious seven-storied building, built with the warm pink brick reminiscent of Florence. "It won't take you more than three minutes to walk there. There is an excellent shopping center opposite the Hospital, and two minutes from your motel. We'll come back in an hour and take you to one of the big self-service stores so that you can stock your larder and then we'll all have supper together somewhere."

They introduced us to our landlord, who escorted us to our apartment on the second floor. We had a large sitting room facing the wide main street, and we looked across to Saint Mary's Hospital, a block away.

I smiled at Nicky. "We'll be close to each other. Perhaps you'll be able to see me sitting here from your bedroom window."

When the Jouberts left us, I intended to unpack our clothes and explore our apartment, but my eyes fell on a pile of letters on the desk, and all else was forgotten. These were the first letters we had received since leaving South Africa and we sat down and read them hungrily.

When they arrived to fetch us, nothing was unpacked, and we had barely looked at our apartment.

They took us to a small restaurant for supper.

Now at last I could ask Peter Joubert all the questions which had been bottled up for so long. Being a doctor and a fellow at the Mayo Clinic, he was able to answer and explain what I wanted to know, which he did with patience and clarity.

He told me about Dr. Abbot.

"You may not like him. Some of his patients who are too garrulous don't get on with him. For instance, he will not be the slightest bit interested that you have brought your son all the way from South Africa for this operation. It makes no difference to him whether you come from Timbuctoo or the house across the road. He is a perfectionist and a completely dedicated man. He has no time for small talk and dislikes being asked a lot of questions."

"All right. I'll ask you a lot of questions instead."

He smiled.

"I was his second assistant for six months and can only describe the feeling I have for him as approaching hero-worship. He is the finest surgeon I have ever seen, and you couldn't have brought Nicky to a better place or placed him in a safer pair of hands."

"Yes. That I know."

"Nicky will never be alone for the first three days he is in the intensive care unit. A specially trained nurse will be with him all the time. During that time Dr. Abbot's first assistant will visit him once an hour, day and night."

"When does he sleep?"

"He doesn't," he said grimly, obviously speaking from past experience.

"This week he will have tests done in preparation for his operation, and you will meet the physicians in Dr. Abbot's team at the Mayo Clinic. You will probably meet Dr. Abbot one or two days before the operation."

He handed me a yellow envelope.

"In here you will find a card for Nicky's appointment at nine o'clock tomorrow morning. It is only a few blocks from your apartment and Nicky should be able to walk there. It is in the same street you are living in. Before we drop you tonight, we'll take you to the Clinic, and I'll show you exactly where you must hand in Nicky's card."

Nicky was in fine fettle. It was obvious he had taken a great liking to this young couple. He was talking too loudly and too much.

We discussed many things: the tests Nicky would have done, the hospital, the operation.

"How long will it take?"

"It varies; it usually takes from four to five hours. Dr. Abbot will send his first assistant to let you know when the crucial stage of the operation is over. You won't see him until the evening. He performs four open heart operations a day, three times a week; and the next week he will perform four a day, twice a week."

"So I won't know until that night whether the operation has been successful."

"It will be successful. Dr. Abbot has performed many operations on Transposition of the Great Vessels with brilliant success."

"It's going to be a long day. I don't know what I shall do
to pass the time. I won't be able to read. I shall probably write
letters all day."

"Yes!" said Nicky in a loud voice. "Write and tell Dad—
the game is on!"

We all laughed. It was time to leave. They drove us down
to the Mayo Clinic. The ten-storied building was a cold, massive block of silvery grey marble. We took the elevator to the
fifth floor, turned right and saw the long desk; the large room,
filled with row upon row of empty chairs, upholstered in soft
green leather. This was where we would come tomorrow. I had
the yellow envelope with Nicky's appointment card safely
tucked in my bag. They drove us home.

Now for the first time I took stock of the apartment where
I was going to spend so many lonely and anxious hours. I liked
what I saw. The wall-to-wall-carpeted sitting room was bright,
airy, and comfortably furnished. There were a sofa and two
easy chairs upholstered in nut brown. A standard lamp stood
next to the desk and there were two more lamps on the occasional tables at each end of the sofa. The curtains were of soft
gold. There were a couple of incredibly hideous ashtrays, and
television for Nicky.

The kitchenette was a small alcove. There was a dining
room table with three chairs, a four-plate stove, a refrigerator
which I was touched to find Sheila Joubert had stocked with
food, and a pop-up toaster. The cupboards were well stocked
with silverware, dishes, pots and pans.

The bedroom was small, with large built-in cupboards.
There was a table between the beds on which stood a small
reading lamp. The covers were nut-brown and the curtains gold.
There was also a tiny pink bathroom.

While Nicky looked at television, I quickly unpacked and

put our things away. We were tired and went to bed early. We both felt happier. We liked the Jouberts, our apartment, and what we had seen of Rochester. I was greatly relieved to have at last reached our final destination and to know that tomorrow the cogs in the wheels would start to turn.

CHAPTER 3

THE next morning I rose early and made a pot of tea. This was to be our daily routine until Nicky left me to go to the hospital. He lay in bed, while I sat on the edge of mine; we nibbled a biscuit and sipped our tea, talking about the Jouberts, Greystones, everything except what was most on our minds. I allowed him to lie in bed while I bathed, then turned him out, and while he was bathing and getting dressed, I made the beds and prepared our breakfast.

It was bitterly cold when we left our apartment; an icy wind was blowing, and it was snowing lightly. As we stepped onto the walk, Nicky pulled up the hood of his anorak and plunged his gloved hands into his pockets. The path stretched in a straight line before us and we immediately saw the cold grey block of the Mayo Clinic on the left. We walked past little wooden houses with no fences dividing them; the green grass stretched in an unbroken verge along the edge of the road. As we slowly approached our austere-looking destination, I saw that the side of the building facing us was a solid block of marble without a window breaking its facade. Nicky tired quickly, and I soon realized, short as the distance was, it was too far for him. After frequent pauses, we reached the door of the Mayo Clinic and I pushed it open, grateful for the gush of warm air which flowed over us.

We took an elevator to the fifth floor and turned to the right. Here, at the long desk, we found a white-uniformed woman who greeted us with a smile as she took Nicky's card, telling us to sit down and wait until our names were called.

The room filled rapidly; a steady stream of people poured in, reported at the desk, and sat down. It was hot and stuffy. Soon we stripped off our coats and sweaters.

Every few minutes a nurse appeared at either the right or left side of the desk, calling the name of a patient. Someone quickly joined her and they disappeared from view, and everyone sat back and relaxed until her next appearance.

At last, after a long interval, we heard "Nicolas Muller." Gathering our possessions, we followed the nurse down a long passage and were ushered into an empty, sparsely furnished room. There were a desk, a chair, and a small uncomfortable sofa. A few medical diplomas hung on the wall; otherwise it was completely impersonal.

Time dragged as we waited for someone to appear.

Nicky sat on the sofa, reading his book. I stood at the window, watching the snowflakes eddying and drifting in the wind. I turned around as the pediatrician entered the room. She was slim, elegant, and coolly efficient. She examined Nicky thoroughly; asked me questions, filled in a lengthy form, and handed me four cards for further tests that day.

I sat waiting for him in the hall while he had X rays taken. We trailed over to the Plummer Building to have an electrocardiograph done. Here again, the room was packed with people, and we sat down, waiting our turn.

It was now well past noon. Nicky's next appointment was at two o'clock and there was not time to return home. He looked tired and depressed. We found a small self-service restaurant near the Clinic. The food was unappetizing, and we were both too strained to eat. By the end of this long day, Nicky was in tears, and I in low spirits.

Our apartment was like a haven when we returned to it. He switched on the television and I took off my shoes and prepared tea and toast.

While we were drinking our tea, I said to him:

"We mustn't allow ourselves to be depressed, Nicky. After all, we knew from the start that it would be like this. We know you must have lots of tests done, and some of them will be unpleasant. We also know that there will be many hours of boredom and must accept all this as part of the adventure."

He nodded and smiled.

At that moment there was a knock on the door. A young boy was standing on the threshold, holding a vase of flowers with a note attached to it.

I thanked him, placing the vase on the desk, and tore the envelope open.

It was a note from Bill's staff welcoming us to Rochester and wishing us luck. I stood holding it, so deeply touched that my eyes filled with tears. I glanced at Nicky. He was looking up at me, grinning like a hyena.

"Don't you dare laugh at me, you little horror."

He gave a loud guffaw and came across the room to hug me.

It was Friday and we now had the weekend before us. There would be no tests for two days. His operation was due to take place on the following Friday.

On Saturday afternoon, Sheila Joubert called for us in their Volkswagen and took us to the largest store in Rochester. Nicky methodically made a list of all his purchases.

The women serving in the shops were friendly and interested. They all knew of Dr. Abbot—he was from their own town, the boy who had made good—and they were immensely proud of him: proud too, that I should travel halfway across the world to place my son in his hands. His name was legend and he was regarded with awe.

During the weekend the Jouberts invited us to dinner and took us to have morning tea with two young friends. We had Sunday lunch with them on the edge of the lake and watched the mallard ducks waddling across the road or sitting in pairs at the edge of the water in the pale sunshine. We saw a pair of Canada geese with an early fledgling, hiding themselves in a sheltered corner of the lake.

A few residents in Rochester had been advised when Nicky and I would be in the city; we had hardly arrived before they telephoned me and tried to arrange a game of bridge. These people were hospitable and kind, in the spontaneous way Americans have.

Everywhere we went, we were conscious of the immense pride and affection the people of Rochester had for their two famous sons, the Mayo Brothers: Charlie, gay and friendly; Will, austere and remote. So many people we met knew them and told us human and amusing anecdotes about them. The regard and love they had for each other we witnessed in every photograph, portrait and statue we saw of them. By the time we left this city, I too felt affection for these two men.

On Monday morning we had an appointment with Dr. Lance, the senior physician in Dr. Abbot's team. Our meeting was brief, as he wished to study the results of the different tests and peruse the catheterization report which had been sent from Cape Town.

He spoke glowingly of Dr. Abbot's immense ability and the brilliant results he had achieved, particularly with Transposition of the Great Vessels.

"He operates on people from all over the world, and from every stratum of life—every race or creed.

"Dr. Abbot and I will meet you tomorrow and he will discuss the operation with you."

He paused.

"As you know, the operation takes place on the eighteenth."

"Not the eighteenth," I quavered. "The fifteenth."

"I am almost certain it is the eighteenth."

"And I am equally certain it is on the fifteenth. That was the date arranged three months ago."

He raised his eyebrows, looking doubtful.

"Just a moment."

He picked up the receiver.

After a few minutes' conversation, during which I sat on the edge of my chair tense with strain, he replaced it.

"It is the eighteenth."

I groaned in anguish. It was like a prison sentence. Three more days of waiting. Another interminable weekend.

I felt like weeping.

Before returning to our appointment we walked over to the big building of the Kahler Hotel. I found Western Union and sent a cable to Bill.

"OPERATION POSTPONED TO EIGHTEENTH STOP NO COMPLICATIONS STOP BOTH FLOURISHING STOP SEND LOTS LOVE EVERYBODY"

For Nicky it was a reprieve. He was happy and smiling.

"Nicky," I said, "aren't you sorry the operation has been postponed until Monday?"

"No." He smiled. "Now I can be with you longer and eat lots of hot dogs."

He wrote to Dirk.

"Dear Dirk,

How are you? Today was a ghastly day. I had to have two blood injections. They are very saw. I have been buying lots of presents lately. It's a damned nuisance. By the way, how did you enjoy your holiday with Olie and Willie, and Mom asks if you went to the Cronises because she has a horrible suspicion you didn't. I am now in Rochester. It's a very nice place. Gosh, but the Mayo Clinic is big all its floors from 1-10 are all made from marble. It must have cost a packet to build. There is still a lot of snow in Rochester. You would like snow very much, it's very cold.

I suppose by the time you will have got this letter I would have had my operation already. Oh, by the way, I have got some very nice flying badges. I got them from the trip up. There is one T.W.A. one, and a PANAM one.

I have got a nice American haircut which is very short and bristly. It's called a flat top. Sue would like it very much.

I suppose you have heard that my operation has been postponed to the eighteenth. What a damn nuisance. Last night Mom made fried chicken for supper 'Mmmmm' it was delicious.

Well I must be ending off now, so give my love to Dad, Sue, Gran and Ed.

Adios for now

Nicky."

After lunch Sheila Joubert took us to Saint Mary's Hospital. Patients from the Mayo Clinic were sent to one of the four private hospitals in Rochester; none were owned by the Clinic, but all were under the direction of its staff members. Of these, Saint Mary's was the largest; in actual fact, the largest private hospital in the United States. It was run by the nuns with efficiency and complete dedication.

When we entered the cardiac unit, my pulse unwittingly quickened. We walked down a wide corridor. A slender nun was speaking to a nurse; she paused as we walked past, and Sheila stopped and introduced us to her.

"Sister Lowell, this is Mrs. Muller and her son Nicky. Dr.

Abbot is operating on him next Monday morning for Transposition of the Great Vessels."

I was taut and nervous.

She smiled at me, and it was as though she laid her cool hand on my febrile spirit and said "Be still."

She greeted us gently. She had a fine Roman nose and her face was sweet and strong. As we walked down the passage, she softly drew my attention to a little girl who was walking in front of us, holding her father's hand.

"She is eight years old, and had Nicky's operation six days ago."

"Six days ago!" I cried in disbelief.

She nodded, smiling gently.

I looked at the little girl as we passed; her cheeks were delicately pink and she was smiling at something her father had said; her lips were still parted in a half-smile as she looked up at me.

We followed Sister Lowell into the intensive care unit. Bedrooms lined both sides of a wide corridor, and at the far end a wide desk stood in front of the window. The nurse sitting behind it rose as we approached her.

"This is Nicky Muller. He is undergoing cardiac surgery on Monday. This is his mother."

She smiled and said to Nicky:

"Hi, Nicky. Where do you come from?"

"South Africa."

"South Africa! Say, do they speak English there?"

He grinned.

"Yes."

Sister Lowell turned to me.

"Mrs. Muller, will you wait here for a few minutes. I want to introduce Nicky to one of the patients."

She took his hand, and they disappeared into an adjoining room.

When we were back in our apartment, I said to him:

"What did Sister Lowell show you when you went into the room together?"

"She introduced me to a little boy who had an operation three days ago."

"What did he look like?"

"He looked fine. He smiled at me. He was sitting on the edge of his bed."

"Go on, Nicky. Not sitting on the edge of his bed. You mean, sitting up in bed."

He smiled.

"No, he was sitting on the edge of his bed, and he was as chirpy as anything."

I took his hand.

"Nicky, don't you feel much happier about everything now?"

"Definitely. Mom, what a super hospital. They told me that you can order television for me. May I have it?"

"You may have television the very second you want it. You may look at it all day, if you want to."

Nicky wrote to his father.

"My dear Dad,

How are you.

I am now in Rochester staying with Mom in the Twins Motel.

Today Mrs. Joubert who looks incredibly like Dot, took us round St. Mary's Hospital. She took us to the Cardiac Section where there was a very nice nun, who showed me some children who had had the same operation as I will have. Some of them were quite lively and there was a little girl who was walking around already.

I had the most ghastly day yesterday. We went to the Mayo. Where I had to have a whole lot of tests done. In one of the tests they gave me an injection, which hurt like hell and after a while it all bunged up. It is much better now, but it hurts if you touch it.

We got a lovely big fat letter from Sue today. The newspapers in America are very dull and boring. Mom says she pre-fers our newspapers much better than the American.

Gosh, it feels as though we have been away about two months already. I really miss Greystones and all its animals and people.

It is very cold in Rochester and there is still quite a lot of snow left on the ground. It was also snowing yesterday.

Well I must be ending off now because its supper time. So give my love to Dirk, Sue and Ed and tell Anna I send my best wishes.

Lots of love and a big kiss,

Nick"

That night, for the first time in many months, I slept well.

CHAPTER 4

As soon as he awoke the next morning, Nicky smiled at me and said: "Today we meet Dr. Abbot." Everything had been moving towards this moment. We had heard so much about the man—his brilliance, his dedication, and his personality—that Nicky was now as interested as I was to meet him.

For me, it was a tense watchfulness. How impressed would I be by this doctor into whose hands we had placed our son's life and future?

He entered the room with his second assistant, and Dr. Lance, the physician. We were to find he was never alone. Even in that first minute I saw him, I was struck by his presence; he was small, slight, and wiry, yet he towered over the other people in the room. His short cropped hair was prematurely grey. He wore glasses, and his face was thin, intelligent, and sensitive. His strong hands were the most competent and beautiful that

I have seen, small boned and narrow. Looking at his hands and at the man himself I felt an upsurge of confidence. I had formed a picture of him in my mind, and he was everything I had hoped for.

His manner was courteous, direct, and cool. He shook hands with both of us, then withdrew to a corner and discussed the reports in a low voice with the physician. He examined Nicky briefly.

He looked across at me and said:

"Have you seen Dr. Joubert?"

"Yes. He very sweetly met me at the plane."

No comment.

I cleared my throat.

"Dr. Thomas asked me to give you his regards."

A grunt; the two doctors shuffled their feet.

He turned to Nicky.

"Nicky, will you wait for a few moments in the passage."

Without looking at anybody and keeping his head down, Nicky walked quickly out of the room. I felt a pang as I watched him go.

Dr. Abbot sat down next to me, turned and faced me, speaking very deliberately.

"We have studied the reports and the results of the catheterization, and we fully agree with the diagnosis of your clinic in Cape Town. We feel that an operation should take place and should greatly benefit your son."

"Would it enable him to lead a normal life?"

"Yes."

"How good will he be afterwards?"

He withdrew slightly.

"I can only answer that question after the operation."

There was a pause.

"Does he know all about his condition and the operation? Have you kept him in the picture?"

"Yes. I have told him everything."

"Good. Every operation of this sort naturally carries an element of risk. In Nicky's case we consider his chances are better than nine out of ten."

These were the same words he had used in his letter. Could I ask for more? Surely, with these odds and Nicky's courage, he must win this great battle.

He was very quiet when we returned to our apartment.

"How did you like Dr. Abbot?" I asked him.

He hesitated.

"I was a bit disappointed."

"I wasn't. You probably expected him to be friendly and warm; but he's not made that way, Nicky. You'll probably find you'll get to like him when you know him better. I feel very much happier now that I have met him."

"Will we meet him again?"

"No."

The next time you meet, I thought with a stab of pain, will be in the operating room.

CHAPTER 5

THE next morning Nicky had to have 20 cubic centimeters of blood removed for matching with the heart and lung machine. He found this an unpleasant ordeal and came out of the room tearful and depressed.

He cheered up when we returned to our apartment and found a large number of letters in our letter box. He sat and read them, while I prepared our lunch.

I was busy cooking when the telephone rang.

"Mrs. Muller?"

"Yes."

"We want you to bring Nicky back to the Clinic this afternoon. His blood is so thick that we find that not enough was removed this morning."

I groaned.

"Could you bring him back at about two o'clock this afternoon?"

Nicky's lips quivered and his eyes filled with tears when I told him. I myself was depressed and unduly upset. He had endured so much with quiet stoicism. This extra load was too much for him, and I was unable to uplift his spirits.

We sat through a miserable lunch. Even a hamburger failed to lighten his gloom. We took a taxi to the Clinic and I collected the card at the desk. As we walked over to the Plummer Building, I glanced at it—60 cubic centimeters.

Nicky sat silently next to me. When his name was called, he quickly dashed his hand across his eyes and followed the nurse. When he returned, he was holding a lollipop, and his eyes were red.

We had a final appointment with Dr. Lance. He told us about the hospital, the operation, and the post-operative care. Though Nicky and I had both read about it, and Peter Joubert had told us much, we now listened with intense interest.

He assured Nicky he would feel little pain after the operation, as the opening of the chest severs few muscles. He told him he would have an oxygen mask over his face for the first three days.

"It is there merely to assist you to breathe.

"You may feel some discomfort at first. You will never be alone. There will always be one or two nurses with you to help you, and a doctor will visit you once an hour."

To me he said:

"You will be allowed to visit Nicky once an hour while he is in the intensive care unit. Dr. Abbot likes the relatives to keep constant contact with the patient."

"I've already told Nicky that I shall visit him once an hour, and he thinks it's a very good idea."

Nicky and I smiled at each other.

He nodded.

"I suggest you visit him hourly until nine o'clock; after that it would be pointless, as he'll probably be asleep. You may start your visits again at eight o'clock the next morning.

"This will also enable you to get some rest," he added kindly.

"You may phone the intensive care unit any time during the night, if you want to know how Nicky is getting on."

There was a pause.

"If there are any questions, Mrs. Muller, you want to ask me, please do so. Is there anything you perhaps don't understand or that Nicky is worried about?"

Everything he said was to reassure us and build up our confidence. This same strength had flowed from Dr. Abbot, Peter Joubert, Sister Lowell, and the other doctors whom we had met. They had bolstered up our courage and morale to such an extent that for the last three nights I had slept peacefully, waking in the mornings refreshed and confident.

Nicky and I had grown very close during the last few weeks. Ever since we shared our tears at the beginning of our Great Adventure, he had been demonstrative and affectionate, darting across the room to hug and kiss me if the mood took him, confiding in me, and talking to me as though we were the same age. We had fallen into an easy companionship—I did the cooking, he set the table. I did the washing-up, he did the drying. He decided what I must cook for lunch. Every night he bolted the door of our apartment before he went to bed.

One night he was sitting quietly in his chair, deep in thought.

I said: "What are you thinking about?"

"I was thinking about Dad."

"Then you can be quite sure that he is thinking about you, too, at this moment. So many people are thinking of you, darling, and so many people love you."

Bill wrote:

"I was thinking this evening that Nicky has brought so much love into our lives: love in our home, and love from our friends."

It was true. Even here, alone and cut off from the

1 4 3

people we knew, we were daily reminded in the letters we read of the concern and affection which was felt. It was like a blanket enfolding us. This more than anything gave us the courage and strength to lift our chins and straighten our backs.

The next day, Helen Frazer telephoned me. She had arrived. I knew that she had timed her visit to Rochester to help me over the difficult hurdle I had to face, and I was deeply grateful. Each day she contacted me. Nicky and I often had tea with her; I was always conscious that she was there in the background if I should ever need her. Each day, too, either Peter or Sheila Joubert telephoned us or came to see us.

Time was crawling past on leaden feet. On Friday we went to the Clinic to receive Nicky's entrance card to the hospital. We were given pamphlets.

"Saint Mary's Hospital is truly a little city within a city, with a total population of about 2,500.

"The medical staff of the Mayo Clinic is the medical staff of Saint Mary's Hospital. The two institutions are separate in organization and financial control. In the care of patients, however, there is close cooperation."

We received a special pamphlet from the cardiac unit.

"An average of 75 open heart operations are performed a month."

A word for the anxious relative during surgery.

"Remember. No news is good news."

Now the weekend was upon us, and time was running out. On Saturday morning Nicky awoke sluggish and apathetic. He ate his breakfast listlessly. When we walked to the shopping center, a block away, he trudged with frightening slowness, dragging his feet, his heavy lids hooding his eyes. I put my hand to his cheek and was relieved to find it was cool to the touch. When we returned to our apartment, he complained that he was tired, so I put him to bed and he immediately fell into a deep sleep.

He woke shortly before lunch, dull-eyed and lethargic. All through the meal, he yawned and hardly spoke.

He made only one heartrending comment.

"I'm beginning to get all tensed up."

By six o'clock that evening he was silent and dull. Peter and Sheila Joubert had arranged to take us to the cinema and were calling for us at seven o'clock. I telephoned her.

"I'm very worried about Nicky. He looks as though he is getting sick. I'm afraid we won't be able to go out with you tonight. I have just given him an aspirin and put him to bed."

All night I tossed and turned, full of anxiety and unreasoning fear. On Sunday morning he woke, clear eyed but solemn and strangely quiet. We spent the morning with the Jouberts. We were glad to escape from our room and to have their company. An oppressiveness and self-consciousness had crept into our relationship now that the time when he must leave me was approaching.

Sheila Joubert handed me a sheet of paper.

"I thought you might be interested to see this. It's the schedule for the operations tomorrow. Nicky's name is eighth on the list."

I found his name.

"Nicolas Muller. Room VI. Dr. W. J. Abbot. 8.00 A.M. Transposition of the Great Arteries with atrial septal defect. Repair. Extra-corporeal circulation."

Nicky slept after lunch. At four o'clock I woke him and we listlessly drank our tea. And now it was time for us to leave. I put on my coat and he silently took his anorak and zipped it up. I picked up his little bag, took his hand, and we set out for Saint Mary's Hospital.

There was a fine drizzle, and the day was bleak and cold, like our mood.

We walked hand in hand down the walk, pausing at the traffic lights. A car drew up next to us. One of the passengers looked at Nicky and nudged the man sitting next to him. He turned and spoke to the people sitting behind him. In a moment they were all openly staring at him. He looked pathetic. Cold and strained, his face was purple and his lips nearly black. When he saw they were looking at him, he turned his face away with touching dignity. The light changed to green and we trudged slowly across the road. I gripped his hand hard, trying to steady the tremor in my voice.

"Nicky, that is the last time this will ever happen to you in your life."

He nodded, not looking at me.

We paused many times for him to regain his breath before we reached the entrance hall of the hospital.

The great marble hall was oppressively hot and stuffy. It was filled with people. Patients sat in little huddled family groups throughout the room. I found a place for Nicky and stripped off his anorak and my coat, placing them next to him. I smiled at him. "I'll be back in a few minutes, darling." I walked across the checkered floor to the long desk in the middle of the room. The young man seated behind it greeted me with a friendly smile. From the moment he checked off Nicky's name on the list in front of him, it was as though an immense machine was put into motion.

I filled in forms and spoke to different officials. I entered an office and explained to a nun that my husband had established credit through our bank with the National Bank in Rochester. These funds would be immediately available for settlement of accounts from the hospital.

Everywhere I was met with friendliness and kindness. "Welcome to Saint Mary's" had not merely been an empty phrase.

Half an hour later, I rejoined Nicky. His face was expressionless. When I smiled at him, he attempted to smile back, but it was no more than an upward curve of his lips, while his eyes remained dark.

Ultimately a young man called our names, took Nicky's

bag and anorak, and escorted us to the elevator. We were shown into the room where Nicky was to spend the night. A nurse gave me the little sleeveless gown he was to wear to the operating room, and I helped him put it on. Our conversation was desultory and strained. He was struggling not to cry.

I was relieved to see Peter Joubert walk into the room, and there was an immediate lifting of Nicky's spirits. His pride forced him to hold back his tears now that we were no longer alone.

A moment later an ebullient young man walked briskly into the room and introduced himself.

"I am Dr. Berange. I am Dr. Abbot's first assistant and will be looking after your son."

He was stocky and powerfully built, with a wide smile and a pelt of short cropped, jet black hair. He was gay, warm, and full of Gallic charm.

He joked and laughed with Nicky while he examined him.

When he was finished he nudged Nicky, pointing to Peter Joubert.

"Do you know what he does? He has a little tube, so beeg," measuring off six inches, "and wiz it, he look through his patients' back window—and now he teenks he's a doctor."

It warmed my heart to hear Nicky's loud guffaw.

But soon they were both gone, and we were alone. The time was drawing relentlessly closer when I must leave him. He sat up in bed and began to cry; not noisily, but with the tears silently streaming down his cheeks. I tried to project his mind into the future and all it held for him, but his terrifying ordeal was too close for him to draw any comfort from my words.

When I bent down to kiss him good-by, he put his arms around my neck and clung to me desperately.

It was dark outside and raining hard.

I buried my hands in my pockets and hunched my shoulders against the icy wind.

The driving rain washed the tears from my cheeks.

CHAPTER 6

I KNEW that sleep, given to me like a gift from the gods this last week, would not be bestowed on me this night, nor many nights to come. I dared not take a sleeping tablet for fear I might oversleep and miss seeing Nicky before he entered the operating room.

I rose early the next morning. I had a hot bath and made myself a scalding cup of coffee.

At half past six I walked into his room. He was fretful and in pain. He had been given an injection in his buttocks which had irritated a nerve in his left leg. He was crying and fractious. I rang the bell. When the nurse arrived, she immediately gave him an injection in his arm. In a few moments he calmed down and became drowsy. I sat and held his hand. Occasionally he opened his eyes to reassure himself I was still there.

At quarter past seven a white-coated attendant entered the

room, pushing a wheelchair. When Nicky saw him, he immediately got out of bed without looking at me and climbed into the chair. As he was being pushed down the corridor, he wordlessly held out his hand for me to hold. I tried in these last moments we had together to will every ounce of my love and strength to flow into him through the communication of our two hands.

The attendant stopped at the door where we had to part, and I bent down and kissed Nicky.

"I'll be seeing you soon, darling."

He stared in front of him, biting his lips.

I stood at the door watching the attendant pushing him slowly down the corridor. He never once looked back. His left hand, which I had been holding, was hanging limply over the arm of his chair. His cropped head and slender neck looked pathetically defenseless above his sleeveless gown.

Before I could check it, the forbidden thought sprang into my mind.

"God. Will I ever see him again."

I found a small waiting room where I was allowed to smoke. I sat down, opened my bag, and took out a cigarette. Ever since the days when I played competitive tennis I had never smoked before lunch. Now my tortured nerves were screaming for a cigarette and I inhaled deeply. It made me giddy and light-headed and I derived little satisfaction from it.

Half an hour later a male nurse entered carrying Nicky's little bag and dressing gown. I followed him down to the cardiac unit. He ushered me into the waiting room where I was to spend the next three days.

It was a large, bright, airy room. Brilliant potted azaleas bloomed on the window sill, and pots of tall, chaste St. Joseph lilies gleamed palely next to them. On a square table lay a half-finished jigsaw puzzle. There were chairs and sofas scattered around the room. A group of people sitting in a corner glanced up as I came in. I nodded good morning and walked to the far end of the room, sitting down on the sofa near the window.

A few minutes later Helen Frazer walked into the room and sat down beside me. She was to spend the whole of this long day with me.

As I had foreseen I was unable to read or even play patience. Most of that morning I sat talking quietly to Helen or writing to Bill and my close friends.

The hours were limping past.

After four hours, I became restive and tense. For the last hour I had been expecting someone to walk in and tell me the crucial stage of the operation was over. No one came. Five hours passed. At last I was told he was "off the pump." At least I now knew he was no longer on the heart and lung machine.

Helen persuaded me to lunch with her in one of the small restaurants opposite the hospital. During this time, she quietly reassured me, trying to soothe my mounting alarm. She was able to answer every medical question I asked her with a quiet conviction which did much to restore my confidence. In her endeavor to help me, her own shy reserve thawed, and a warmth crept into our relationship which had not been there before. For her strength and companionship that day she was to earn my lifelong gratitude.

At a quarter past two Dr. Berange walked into the waiting room.

"The operation is over. You may come and see Nicky."

He still wore the white cap and gown from the operating theatre.

"How is he?"

He gave a wide, cheerful smile.

"He's fine!"

I followed him down the passage, listening to the loud clicking of my heels, consciously bracing and steeling myself against what I would see. It was the stuff that nightmares are made of. He looked as though he had been crucified. He was naked and ice-cold. The wound down his chest was covered with adhesive. His small tortured body was stained with mercurochrome. Two tubes were imbedded in his stomach. Two more were planted in his groins and another two sprang from his arms. Two slender tubes were fixed into his nostrils, held by a metal clip attached to the tip of his nose, and two larger ones were strapped into his mouth, hissing oxygen down his throat. He was struggling and fighting against it. I froze with shock. This was something neither of us had expected. His face was hidden under adhesive. Only his eyes were visible, distended and agonized. When he saw me, they crumpled, and I quickly grasped his hand and pressed it against my cheek.

"Remember what I told you, darling. Relax. Try to relax and sleep. Don't fight against anything."

He instantly closed his eyes and lay still.

The only sound in the room was the steady hissing of the oxygen.

The two nurses were busy and cheerful. It was obvious that nothing unusual was taking place.

One of them said:

"Look how pink his hands are."

I picked up his cold flaccid hand and turned it over. The palm was delicately pink.

I pressed it to my lips and quietly stole out of the room. I said to Helen:

"That is a sight which will be branded in my mind forever. Why are there two tubes strapped into his mouth? They told me he would have an oxygen mask over his face."

"They often use the tubes for older children. It helps their breathing immensely and takes a great deal of strain off them. He will probably not use them for more than four or five hours."

"He was fighting against it, because he did not expect it."

"He'll probably accept it very soon; if he doesn't, they'll give him an oxygen mask."

"I think I'll walk to the apartment in case there are letters for me."

I had to escape from the hospital. I walked across to our

motel and my heart lifted when I opened the letter box and saw there were letters from Bill, his mother, and my friends.

I made tea, lit a cigarette, and read them, trying to relax. Ten minutes later, I flung on my coat and walked back to the hospital.

He was lying on his back asleep. The rhythmic sound of the oxygen was no longer frightening. I noticed his toes were pink and the clubbing of his fingertips was much less noticeable. The deep purple padding was now palely pink, and I could see that one day he would have long, slender fingers.

"Why is he so cold?" I asked one of the nurses. "His body is like ice."

"It is very important to keep his temperature down at this stage. Don't worry, he is doing very well."

When I saw him at half past four, he was conscious, breathing gently and cooperating very bravely. He was accepting his discomforts with great courage. When I saw the quiet determination with which he was fighting his battle, my own spirits were uplifted in a great surge of happiness and hope.

At seven o'clock, Dr. Abbot and his team walked into the far end of the waiting room. He sat down next to a young couple and started to speak to them, while the doctors stood in a silent group.

When I saw them moving over towards us, my stomach tied itself into a knot. Helen picked up her bag and quietly slipped out of the room. He sat down next to me, wishing me a courteous good evening. He spoke quietly and deliberately.

"We operated on your son and found everything that we expected and were able to repair his heart successfully."

"Was there anything unusual about the operation?"

I had heard a whisper that there had been something different. I had sensed an excitement amongst the doctors and nurses.

He hesitated.

"We moved and repaired a small vein, which in no way affects the success of the operation."

"Why did he have tubes strapped into his mouth? Is it usually done?"

He looked surprised.

"It is customary to use them."

Now I could ask him the question which he had been unable to answer before.

"What are his future prospects?"

"Very good."

One further question I had to ask him.

"May I send a cable to my husband worded 'Operation *completely* successful'?"

"Yes."

He paused to see if there were any further questions I wished to ask, then rose and said goodnight.

My throat was tight.

I knew how much the word "completely" would mean to Bill.

An hour later, Peter Joubert walked into the waiting room.

"Nicky looks very good. They are very pleased with his condition. Come out with me and have something to eat."

"Do you think I should leave the hospital?"

"It will do you good. We'll go to the intensive care unit and tell them where they can contact us."

When we were in the car, I turned to him.

"What is this mysterious vein everybody is so excited about?"

"It is known as anomalous pulmonary venous drainage. The hole in his heart was too small to keep Nicky alive. This vein, which has now been moved to the correct place, kept him alive, and explains why his condition was so good in spite of his very severe heart disability. It is not uncommon, but it is the first time it has appeared when operating on Transposition of the Great Vessels."

154

"In other words, this little vein really kept him alive!"

"Yes."

He smiled.

"Nicky has made medical history. His name will appear in text books."

"He'll love that."

Later, Dr. de Goede was to write: "Nicky had no hole in the wall between the two ventricles, which was very fortunate for the operation, and no patent ductus connecting the aorta and pulmonary artery. However, we had found at the first catheterization a pulmonary vein from the upper lobe of the right lung, which joined the right atrium, and not the left. This vein, by its abnormal connection, delivered red blood directly into the right side of the heart and probably explained Nicky's remarkable survival. It could be looked upon as Nature's own attempt at cure. In fact the rationale of the surgical procedure in this condition is to switch over the venous connections of the ventricles, thereby making blue blood go to the left ventricle and red blood to the right. By doing this, it no longer matters that the great arteries are transposed.

"I had been very excited about this anomalous v 'n, and in our meetings suggested that this explained Nicky's survival. I was not surprised that the doctors at the Mayo were equally enthralled on finding it and appreciating that it had, in fact, been Nicky's 'vein of life.'"

When we returned to the intensive care unit an hour later, Peter Joubert left me for a moment and came back smiling.

"I've just read Dr. Abbot's report on Nicky. It says 'Condition excellent.'"

Dr. Berange was examining him when I went into his room. When he saw me, he gave his wide, charming smile, and lifted finger and thumb.

I walked across and looked at Nicky.

The tubes had been removed from his nostrils and mouth and a transparent plastic oxygen mask was over his face. For the first time I saw the delicate rosy cheeks and the bright red lips. For the first time I witnessed the miracle of his pinkness, which I was to marvel at afresh each time I saw him.

He opened his eyes and smiled at me, and I smiled back at him, my eyes wet with tears.

As I was leaving the nurse said to me:

"Mrs. Muller, will you write down your address and telephone number, in case we should wish to contact you during the night."

The apartment was cold, empty, and unwelcoming when I entered it. Nicky's sweater was lying on the sofa, and his toys were piled on the writing desk.

I felt a hundred years old. My nerves were stretched to breaking point. I collapsed onto my bed, reveling in its yielding softness and the bliss of lying down. I had never before experienced such fatigue. I tried to relax and quell the feverish turmoil in my mind. Slowly, as the minutes passed, I started to unwind. My legs stopped trembling and the tension left my body. From sheer exhaustion I fell asleep.

The telephone rang. The shrill sound was shocking.

In a second I was wide awake, my heart pounding and my body trembling. I dashed across the room and picked up the receiver.

"Hello," I said, trying to control my fear.

"Is that you, Mary? This is Charles speaking. How is Nicky?"

The words meant nothing to me. I had been so certain the call was from the hospital that my brain, sluggish and numb, seemed incapable of assimilating anything else. I stood clutching the receiver in silence.

"Are you there, Mary? Can you hear me? This is Charles speaking. We want to know how Nicky's operation has gone."

"My God, Charles," I cried. "Do you realize you nearly succeeded in giving me a king-sized heart attack? I thought they were phoning me from the hospital."

"How is Nicky?" he asked, with a tinge of impatience.

"He's wonderful. He is pink and blooming. The operation has been a complete success. Dr. Abbot is very pleased with his condition."

"How marvelous. Here is Anni. She is dying to speak to you."

"Hello, Mary. What wonderful news."

"Yes, isn't it absolutely fantastic. It's like a miracle. I wish you could see what he looks like. It is quite unbelievable."

The full realization of what had happened suddenly flooded my tired brain.

He was not out of the woods yet; there were still two crucial days to go. He was on the danger list—but Nicky was going to be a normal little boy. Everything we had prayed for had come to pass. All our hopes and dreams were coming true. The last black cloud had vanished from our sky, and the sun was shining with blinding brilliance.

CHAPTER 7

I WALKED into Nicky's room at a quarter to eight the next morning. I took off my coat and went over to him. Gently removing the oxygen mask, I bent down and kissed his soft rosy cheek. He smiled, but did not speak.

"Would you like to see what you look like?"

He nodded.

I opened my bag and took out my mirror. At that moment Dr. Abbot walked into the room. I picked up my coat.

"Would you like me to leave?"

"No, you may stay."

He said good morning to Nicky.

"How are you feeling?"

Nicky whispered "Fine."

While he was examining him, he turned to me and said: "He's doing very well."

He moved over to the door to consult with the nurse, and

I went over to Nicky's bed and held up the mirror so that he could see himself.

He stared solemnly and then smiled.

"Don't you look super!"

Dr. Abbot flashed back a smile as he left the room.

I could not take my eyes off Nicky. His face was thinner, and his features more distinct and delicate. His eyes, no longer bloodshot, were clear, the whites gleaming like porcelain. His mouth was red, and his cheeks had a rich peachy bloom.

The adhesive had been removed from his wound. The thread-like incision ran from the base of his throat to two inches above his navel. It was as neat as a zipper and looked clean and healthy.

All day he was plagued by thirst. He was allowed nothing to drink, and his increasing thirst was constant torment to him. Thick mucus congested his chest. Time and again he was painfully propped up and encouraged to cough and get rid of it.

His courage and fortitude were heartbreaking. He fought with quiet determination. His obvious discomfort he bore without complaint and he never cried once. Most of this day he slept. Often I stole in to see him and quietly tiptoed out again, grateful to see his peacefully sleeping face behind the oxygen mask.

Helen tiptoed in to see him.

"He looks wonderful," she said when she rejoined me. "His face has lost that congested, bloated look and his features are more delicate. I think you'll find he will be much brighter and more intelligent."

When I repeated this to Peter Joubert, he snorted in disbelief.

"I can't see how this can possibly affect his intelligence."

However, a couple of months later when Professor Rudolph examined him at the Cardiac Clinic in Cape Town, he said:

"He will be much more intelligent. Have you noticed it?"

"It is difficult for me to judge," I said. "He's not back at school yet."

I spent the day sitting in the waiting room writing letters and noticed a new group of people sitting at the far end of the room. I looked up as a woman sank down on the sofa next to me.

"I believe your son had cardiac surgery yesterday, and that Dr. Abbot operated on him."

I nodded. "Yes."

She spoke English with a French accent.

"He is now operating on our son."

How well I knew her suffering.

A moment later her husband joined us and the rest of that day we sat talking together. They were called Michèle and Louis. They had suffered the same anguish and despair Bill and I had endured all these years, and this formed an immediate bond between us.

"I brought Luke here five years ago, for heart surgery," Michèle said, "and they told me then we would have to bring him back here for open heart surgery when he was six. Now, when he had all the tests done at the Mayo Clinic last week, they found he has a severe abdominal defect and we will have to bring him here again next year for major abdominal surgery. Why does one little boy have to endure so much? Why must everything happen to one child?"

"He has such guts," Louis said proudly. "He has more courage than all the other children put together."

We compared the different tests our children had at the Mayo Clinic.

"Nicky had to have two lots of blood removed for matching with the heart and lung machine," I said. "His blood was so thick that they removed too little the first time."

"We had exactly the same experience with Luke," Louis said. "They urged us to bring him here when he reached the age of six, as his heart was manufacturing such thick blood that there was the danger of his having a stroke."

Often during the day Michèle or Helen and I slipped out of the exit door and sat on the cold and grimy staircase. This dismal and gloomy spot was the only place where smoking was permitted in the cardiac unit. One tall metal ashtray stood at the foot of the stairs, filled to the brim with half-smoked cigarettes. Here a motley array of smokers gathered, standing at the door, or at the window half-way up the stairs, or crouched on the stairs themselves.

The next day I wrote to Bill: "I walk around with a permanent smile on my face. I have not felt like this for ten years. In fact, I don't think I have ever felt so humbly grateful or as happy as I do at this moment. Nearly all the horrible tubes have been removed, excepting for the one in his right arm; and this morning, for the first time, Nicky had a little orange juice and has been allowed to drink water."

I took Michèle in to see him.

"Oh, Neeky! You are so beautiful!"

I stole in to see Luke. He lay and stared at me solemnly. I liked his small freckled face and stubborn chin.

I spent all day in the hospital. The apartment became a place where I only ate and slept. Loneliness had me in her cold grip. I missed Nicky. I missed his company, his warmth. Now, when I entered our room at night, a pall fell on my spirits.

I was able to buy all my provisions from the shopping center opposite the hospital. I found fruit, meat and vegetables exorbitantly expensive. Now that Nicky was no longer with me, I ate very little, not because the food was expensive, but because I had no appetite and was too lazy to cook myself a proper meal. I lived on soup, eggs, and toast, taking the minimum time to eat, quickly returning to the desk and writing letters far into the night.

I found two dominant traits in all my dealings with Americans, whether it was at the Mayo Clinic or in a store: I always met with impeccable politeness and streamlined efficiency.

I wrote to Bill: "They are the most polite people I have ever met!"

On the fourth day Nicky was moved out of the intensive care unit to his own room. This was a great day for both of us. He was off the danger list.

His room was bright and sunny. He had his own bathroom, a writing desk, and a telephone next to his bed, and I immediately ordered television for him. Now I could sit with him all day.

Michèle came in to see him.

"Oh, Neeky! You are beautiful! It makes me feel better just to look at you."

Half an hour later when I joined her on the staircase, she was drawn and pale.

"They have just told us that Luke had a stroke last night."

My heart contracted.

"It happened at two o'clock this morning. They tell me that Dr. Berange sat with him for two hours. For that I will always love him. Why must everything happen to Luke? He is only six."

I tried to comfort her, but she was too deeply distressed to derive solace from words.

"They tell us it was not a severe stroke. They don't know yet how much damage has been done. Six neurologists have seen him and poor little Luke just lies there, he never smiles."

We walked up the corridor together.

"I am going to see Luke now. May I come and sit with you and Neeky sometimes?"

"Please do!" I said warmly. "We would love to have you. Nicky is very fond of you."

But she came only once, wearing dark glasses, distrait and despairing.

Now I knew what was behind the door which I had kept locked and bolted in the past. Nicky would have had a stroke. His thick, congested blood would have destroyed him far sooner than any of us anticipated.

The telephone rang early the next morning.

It was Nicky.

"Bring my robe and slippers," he ordered. "I am going to walk today."

"Ay, ay, sir! Is there anything else you want?"

"Yes. Hurry up!"

When I walked into his room, he was having a bath. His thin bruised body was horrifying. A broad, pale-blue band surrounded the incision down his chest. There were two deep red indentations in his stomach and black bruises in his groins. For the first time I saw the seven-inch wound in his right thigh, which was purple to the knee.

"My God," I exclaimed in horror. "He looks as though he has been hit by a truck."

"That is more or less what has happened to him," said Dr. Berange. "He has been taking medication to thin his blood, and this causes the bruising to become more lurid."

"What is that dreadful wound on his leg?"

"Some of the sheath of the thigh muscle was used to repair his heart."

"Will it grow again?" I asked fearfully.

"Of course."

Nicky and I walked down the passage; he limped because his thigh was painful, but nevertheless he was walking better than he had ever done before.

Now that he was on his feet, the difference in his appearance was more marked than ever. His face had fined down, and he bore a striking resemblance to his father. In any company he would have looked healthy; but here, in a country where most of the children I had seen were pale, his brilliant complexion was almost startling, and his air of good health and toughness was emphasized by his short cropped hair.

As we walked down the passage, people involuntarily smiled when he passed them.

He wrote to his father.

164

"My dear Dad,

Thank you so much for your two very kind letters. I am getting on wonderfuly well here in hospital. I must admit that after the op. I felt a little uncomfortable, but now I feel like a million dollars so please dont worry about me. I have just been downstairs to the basement of the hospital to have a coke. Please thank Dirk for his very funny letter. Tell him I laughed myself till I almost got sick. What a sweet little squirrel Squidie must be and how Carlos would love to eat him.

It is very nice because every time Mom goes home I can watch her from the hospital window and I can see her sitting-room window and I can see her inside.

This hospital is very nice, but the food isn't so very good. My room is very comfortable. Its got a big arm chair, a couple of other stools and a T.V. set. Mom eats very little now that I am not there. She usually just has a piece of toast and a cup of hot coffee and she says that flat feels very lonely when she goes home at night.

Well Dad, I must be ending off now. So give my love to Dirk, Sue and Ed, and of course also to Gran.

Lots of love and a big kiss from your healthy son,

Nick"

CHAPTER 8

THE next day I took Nicky to visit Luke, who was now in his own room, opposite ours. Nicky was sitting in a wheelchair, holding a present for Luke in one hand and Freda in the other. Freda was a toy dachshund which Sheila Joubert had given him. On her right ear was written "My Nurses," on her left ear "My Doctors," and on her body "My Visitors."

When I pushed Nicky into the room and Luke saw him, a smile lit up his face.

Michèle cried: "Oh, Luke! That is the first real smile you have given since you've been in hospital. Neeky! You have made him give a proper smile."

"Will you sign your name on Freda?" Nicky asked, handing the dog to her.

She signed her name, then looked at the other signatures with interest.

"I see you haven't got Dr. Abbot's signature."

"Somehow I can't picture Dr. Abbot signing his name on Freda's ear," I said.

"I want to sign my name!" cried Luke.

He seized Freda, turned her upside down, and started to write his name on her belly, but his fingers were unable to control the pencil. Determined, but bewildered, he persevered; then he stopped trying. The smile left his face, and he stared blankly in front of him. The pencil hung loosely between his limp fingers. Michèle's face was drawn and her eyes desperate.

Many times during the day, Nicky and I walked down the passage, hand in hand. He was walking with a pronounced limp and it was soon obvious that his thigh was extremely painful.

When Dr. Abbot and the doctors came to visit him that evening, he was in bed, sitting erect and looking so ludicrously healthy that they all started to laugh. When Dr. Abbot finished reading the day's report, he rose and stood at the foot of Nicky's bed, smiling at him.

"He's perfect!" he said, briefly raising his slender hand.

The next day Nicky was completely immobilized. The thigh was burning, turgid, and deeply purple. This setback was too much for him; his courage deserted him and he wept with pathetic abandon. I, too, was unutterably depressed, irrationally incapable of accepting this reverse.

It was now a week since his operation had taken place, and we had both foolishly hoped he would join me in our apartment by the end of the week.

"Will I be able to go home on Thursday?" he asked, quivering piteously.

"I don't know, darling. After all, we don't even know whether that is the day you will be allowed to go home."

The tears ran down his cheeks.

"When will I be able to walk again?"

I looked at his grossly swollen thigh. I gently laid my hand on it, feeling its burning heat.

"It won't be very soon. Nicky, don't let this upset you too much. The thing that really matters is you are now healthy and strong. You've got your whole life in front of you. What does it matter if you stay in the hospital for a few extra days?"

He sobbed uncontrollably.

Dr. Berange explained to us what had happened.

"The medication which Neeky has taken to thin his blood has caused the wound in his thigh to bleed internally. It doesn't usually happen. He has been unlucky. You must stay in bed today, Neeky. Don't try to use your leg."

"Will I be able to go home on Thursday?" he wailed.

"We'll see when the time comes. Neeky, this isn't important. You're a normal healthy boy now, that is what matters."

"When will I see Dr. Abbot?"

"You will see him this evening."

He pulled himself together. He asked me to give him a tissue and tragically wiped his eyes and blew his nose.

I hardly left his side that day. I even avoided Michèle's company and sympathy. I knew that tomorrow I would be better adjusted.

On returning to my apartment for lunch, I found the letter box overflowing with letters from South Africa. They were the first of many I was to receive expressing joy and relief at the success of Nicky's operation.

I glowed with happiness. Settling myself in a comfortable chair, I lit a cigarette and tore open the first letter. Before reading half the paragraph, I burst into tears, tears which did not cease to flow until I had read the last letter half an hour later. It was like the bursting of a dam; a release of tension which left me weak, tired and relaxed.

Bill wrote: "What a wonderful relief to get your cable, and how well you worded it! I was down at the garage just after nine o'clock this morning, filling up with petrol, when I was told that a cable had arrived for me at the office. You can imagine my feelings before opening it. This was probably one

169

of the worst moments of my life—and then the absolute joy of seeing that the operation had been a complete success. I am afraid the tears streamed down my cheeks and I was unable to go and tell the staff for quite a while."

His mother wrote: "Thank God. What wonderful news. I wept, my tears have been so bottled up, I let them flow. What a relief for you. My thoughts have been with you always."

And from Sue: "Dad phoned me this morning with the wonderful, wonderful news. Oh Mom, I just can't get over it. I'm afraid the tears were pouring down my face after Dad told me, and I had to dash to the cloakroom to control myself and wash my face. Even though one is confident and tries to make oneself believe that it will be a success, there is still that knowledge that something could go wrong, or that perhaps the condition was more complicated than they originally thought. Poor Dad sounded quite beside himself with joy. I've never heard him like that before; he was positively shouting over the phone."

I took the letters back to Nicky.

He read of the love and admiration our friends felt for him. He read how his father, grandmother, and sisters wept tears of joy on his behalf. He read of the sympathy felt for the trials he had endured, and the delight expressed at the miracle which had taken place.

He read a letter from Bill's cousin.

"We've just received the wonderful news and I doubt if there is a single member of our vast family who on hearing it managed to stay completely dry eyed. As I said to Aunt Mary just now, it's like hearing of a new birth in the family—only of course it is even more joyful than that—because we all know and love Nicky and so it's more meaningful."

When he had finished reading the last letter his face was glowing and his eyes were deeply bright. For the rest of the afternoon he was quiet and happy, apparently resigned to being confined to his bed.

A dramatic change took place when Dr. Abbot and the

team of doctors walked into his room that evening. As soon as he saw Dr. Abbot he started to cry, but not the heart-broken, pathetic sobs of the morning. Now he was an actor in the center of the stage, commanding the full attention of his audience.

"What is wrong, Nicky?" Dr. Abbot asked with charming concern.

"It's my leg," he said. "I can't walk."

Now I was to witness the gentleness and tenderness of this austere and dedicated man.

"Nicky, I cannot tell you how very, *very* sorry I am this has happened," he said with such sincerity that I found a lump in my throat.

Meanwhile Nicky cast a sharp glance in my direction, indicating that he wanted something. I glanced around and behind me, not knowing what it was he wanted.

"When will I be able to walk again?"

"Nicky, I want you to keep absolutely quiet for the next two days."

"When will I be able to go home?"

Nicky shot me another exasperated look and irritably pointed his finger. A doctor who was standing close by picked up Freda, who was standing on the desk behind me, and gave her to him.

Talking and crying, Nicky now held her a foot from Dr. Abbot's nose.

We were all smiling. The doctors were smiling, Sister Lowell was smiling, Dr. Abbot was smiling.

He took Freda and wrote his name on her left ear.

"Wouldn't you like to have the signature of a famous surgeon from Paris?"

Nicky nodded.

The famous surgeon from Paris stepped forward with a broad smile and signed his name.

"And now, what about a well known doctor from Israel? Your dog is going to be very valuable."

When they all trooped out of the room, Nicky sat upright in bed, examining his new signatures with interest.

A moment later Dr. Berange returned.

He put his arms around Nicky, enfolding him in a warm, affectionate, and protective embrace. He pressed his face against Nicky's cheek. His short black hair was like the soft dark fur of an animal.

"Don't worry, Neeky. You will still leave the hospital at the same time. Your leg is not going to make any difference."

He had hardly left when Sister Lowell glided into the room carrying a large glass of Coke.

"Have a good cry, Nicky. You have been so brave, you haven't cried once. Have a cry; it will do you good."

CHAPTER 9

THE days passed slowly. I spent eight hours a day with Nicky. When I mentioned this to a friend back in South Africa, she said: "Good heavens. Why eight hours!" "Because he wanted it," I said. "It was the only thing I could do for him. He liked me to be there, even if he was reading or looking at T.V., and he was very grateful. He never took it for granted."

One morning Sister Lowell introduced me to a young couple. I was immediately struck by their drawn appearance.

"Mrs. Muller, I want you to meet Mr. and Mrs. Ashton. Dr. Abbot is operating on their son for Transposition of the Great Vessels."

"He's a marvelous surgeon," I said. "He operated on my son six days ago for the same complaint, and now he looks absolutely wonderful. I still can't believe it."

Sister Lowell gave a little smile as she quietly slipped away and left us, knowing that at this moment I could comfort them more than anyone else.

Whenever I met them, I always inquired about their little son, and after a few days I saw them pushing him in a wheelchair down the passage.

One morning I was sitting on the stairs smoking when the father joined me.

"Isn't it wonderful," I said, "to know that your son now has a future and will be able to lead a normal life."

"Our son won't be able to lead a normal life," he said quietly. "They were not able to help him as much as your boy."

I was speechless, bitterly regretting my words.

Nicky's leg mended slowly. For two days he was unable to move; then slowly and painfully he forced himself to walk. The leg was still swollen and badly discolored. When he put his weight on it, it was agonizing.

I wrote to Bill: "This afternoon a young nurse took Nicky down to the library in a wheelchair. He refused any assistance. He got out of bed by himself, steeled himself, and with difficulty limped over to the wheelchair. With obvious great pain, he managed slowly to hoist himself into it. When we were walking down the passage, the nurse turned to me and said, 'Your son has great courage for a small boy.'"

With grim determination he was literally fighting to get on his feet again, so that he could leave the hospital by the end of the week.

Every day he asked Dr. Berange when he would be allowed to go home, but our Gallic friend remained noncommittal.

"May I go home on Saturday?"

"We will see. Maybe."

He received constant care and attention. His blood pressure was taken three times a day. Five doctors, including Dr. Abbot and Dr. Berange, visited him twice daily, writing their reports, which were kept in a folder outside his door. In the evening when he paid his final visit, Dr. Abbot brought the reports in with him and studied them.

174

"Am I allowed to read the reports?" I asked one of the doctors.

"Definitely not!" He smiled. "Some time ago, Dr. Abbot was operating, and during a pause, he slipped on a dressing gown and went up to the cardiac unit to check on a patient about whom he was worried. He was standing in the corridor reading the reports when a nurse who had only just started in the unit rushed across and snatched it out of his hand, saying 'Patients are not permitted to read the reports.' Sister Lowell, who was there when it happened, smiled and said, 'Don't you know who that is?' When the little nurse realized what she'd done, she was covered in confusion."

"What did Dr. Abbot do?"

"He was very amused."

Sister Lowell visited Nicky four times a day. Every night she glided into his room to say goodnight to him.

We saw a great deal of Michèle, Louis, and Luke.

I said to them: "Meeting the three of you has been the nicest thing that has happened to me in Rochester."

Usually when I arrived at the hospital in the morning, I found Nicky sitting in his wheelchair in Luke's room, talking to them.

Every day I saw Louis or Michèle walking down the passage holding Luke's hand. He dragged his right foot slightly, but the movement was practically imperceptible, and looking at his small, strong face, I had a feeling of confidence that in time he would overcome this disability. Louis gave him a gun, and with painstaking resolution he taught himself to pull the trigger with his right hand. Now he trotted down the passage, shooting everybody at sight, his face wreathed in smiles.

I invited the Jouberts and Michèle and Louis to dinner. I booked a table at what I was told was the smartest restaurant in Rochester.

We were handed over-sized menus.

Peter Joubert stared at his with open-mouthed consternation.

I nudged him and said in Afrikaans:

"Stop trying to find the cheapest thing on the menu! Order something wildly extravagant. This is a party to celebrate the most wonderful thing that has ever happened in my life. Here's to Nicky!"

When we set out upon our Great Adventure I had anticipated the chill embrace of loneliness. I had neither sought nor expected companionship and friendship—yet, I had found it.

When I walked into Nicky's room on Friday morning, Dr. Berange had just finished examining him.

"May I go home tomorrow?"

Dr. Berange turned to me.

"We have found that Neeky has put on two pounds in two days. This means that he is retaining liquid and his liver has become enlarged."

Seeing my alarmed expression, he said soothingly:

"This happens to 90 percent of the patients who have Transposition of the Great Vessels and we have been expecting it."

He turned to Nicky and said kindly:

"This was why I didn't want to tell you what day you could go home, Neeky."

Nicky was crying bitterly.

"We have put him on Digitalis, and tonight we will give him medication to make him urinate frequently. We cannot allow him to go home until his condition is stabilized."

"But when may I go home?" Nicky cried pitifully.

Dr. Berange sat on the edge of his chair and looked at Nicky with stern affection.

"The most important thing is that you must be absolutely well before you leave the hospital. If you leave too soon, all the good work could be undone. You wouldn't want that to happen, would you?"

Nicky shook his head, wiping the tears away with his hand.

"You will be sensible now, won't you? You've got so much to look forward to. What are a few days in a lifetime?"

176

But he was inconsolable when Dr. Berange left.

Peter Joubert came to see us an hour later. Nicky was red-eyed and miserable. Sensing my fear, he explained to us carefully and in great detail what had occurred.

"Most patients who have open heart surgery are put on Digitalis. Nicky may have to take it for several months. Some of the older patients take it for years. It is quite harmless. You or I could take it without ill effect. They are giving it to Nicky to assist his heart. The fact that his liver has enlarged and he is retaining liquid is an indication his heart is not functioning properly. The right ventricle is doing two-thirds more work than it has ever done before, and the left ventricle two-thirds less. It will take his heart a bit of time to adapt itself to these new pressures and strains. They will stabilize his condition and he will take Digitalis until such time as your physician in Cape Town decides that his heart will be able to function normally without assistance."

He told me that when Nicky joined me in our apartment, he would have to be on a salt-free sodium-free diet. Lack of salt presented no problem, as in Rochester I would have no difficulty obtaining salt-free bread and butter.

Sodium was the fly in the ointment. No canned foods, no cakes, cookies or sweets, no frozen vegetables, no commercial ice creams or jellies.

"How long does this diet last?"

"Usually two or three weeks; then he will be put on a much milder diet, where he may have a little salt cooked in his food and will be allowed to eat ice cream and cake."

"I'm sorry, darling," I said to Nicky. "I won't be allowed to give you those two hot dogs I promised you for your first meal."

By the next morning Nicky had accepted his reverse philosophically.

"Actually, Mom, my leg has been a blessing in disguise. Otherwise I may have left the hospital too soon."

Before the day was over, it was found that Luke, too, was retaining liquid.

Michèle and Louis moved into the apartment next to ours. Just as the mists rise from the valley in the warmth of the morning sun, so did the last chill wisps of my loneliness dissipate. Luke was going home on Sunday.

When I arrived at the hospital that morning, I found Nicky sitting with Luke, Michèle, and Louis. Michèle was slowly packing his clothes and toys into a suitcase, and Louis was assembling a trout rod.

As soon as he saw me, Nicky said:

"I have got good news for you. Dr. Berange says that I may go home on Tuesday."

I hugged him. It was the first time Dr. Berange had committed himself.

"He says I've responded very well to the medication."

He wrote to Bill.

"My dear Dad,

How are you? I am feeling wonderful here in hospital and have got only two more days in hospital. My stitches are now out and my chest feels very much more comfortable. There were 32 in my chest, 16 in my leg and eight in groin, which makes 56 altogether, which isn't bad. Luke Sheid has left the hospital for the Twins and he is happy to be out of hospital.

Last night the Sheids took Mom to a flick, which she enjoyed very much. They have been very nice to us. Dr. Abbott is very nice, and I like him very much.

I have just had supper and it is now six o'clock, but South African time it is one o'clock at night. I had roast veal, a baked potatoe and a bowl of canned cherries for supper. It wasn't bad.

Down in the basement of the hospital there are a whole lot of machines, where you can get sandwiches, cool drinks, chocolate etc. You just put a coin in a slot, push a button and out pops whatever you want. I can go down there at any time and get something to eat or drink.

I must say I am getting pretty sick of this hospital. I've

been here over two weeks now. I'm sorry I can't give you much news when I am cooped up in a little room the whole day, so I hope you don't find my letter to boring. I will carry on with this letter in the morning seeing there is no more news for today.

7:15 P.M.

I have just had a very good supper. Sheila Joubert has just been in to see me. She has been very kind to me lately. She looks so much like Dot that when she came in the day before yesterday I thought that Dot had flown all the way down from Bulawayo to see me.

I will be going home tomorrow, and I am very pleased.

Mom has just gone out for a smoke. She has to sit in the most ghastly little place. She says its quite enough to put her off smoking for quite a long time, but nevertheless she still goes every few hours.

Dirk's squirrel sounds to sweet for words. I only hope it will still be alive when I reach Cape Town. It hasn't got much hope with Carlos prowling around.

Dad please give Keith Maxwell my regards when you see him and tell him to tell all my friends that I am getting on fine and will be back soon.

Well, I better be ending off now. So give my love to Dirk, Sue, Ed and a special big kiss for you

from Nick"

Now, when I returned to our apartment for lunch, or when I came back in the evening, I was no longer alone. I had the warmth and companionship of Louis, Michèle, and Luke. I was waiting with consuming impatience for Nicky to join us.

On Tuesday morning when I walked into his room we both smiled.

"Well, Nicky, all the worst part of the Great Adventure is now over. This is really the beginning of your new life."

I packed his bag and was helping him to get dressed when Dr. Berange walked in.

"I teenk I examine you, Neeky, to see if you are fit enough to go home today."

Nicky rolled an apprehensive eye in his direction. There was a delighted burst of laughter, and Nicky was enfolded in two strong affectionate arms.

"You must take him to the Clinic every day until you leave. Here is an appointment card for his visit tomorrow. Dr. Abbot and I will see him on Thursday."

"When will we be allowed to return to South Africa?"

"Dr. Abbot will tell you."

I was sent down to the pharmacy to collect his Digitalis, his pills "for the waterworks," and his vitamins.

When I returned a nurse meticulously measured each dose in front of me and gave it to Nicky, demonstrating exactly how it should be administered.

We went hand in hand to say good-by to Sister Lowell and to all his nurses who had looked after him with such infinite care and gentleness.

We walked into the intensive care unit to say good-by to the nurses who had looked after him for the first three crucial days.

"I love my work," one of them said, looking at Nicky. "It is so rewarding. It is such a wonderful feeling to know that we are doing good and have contributed towards giving someone a new life."

Michèle arrived and helped me to carry Nicky's things.

We went down in the elevator for the last time. The sun was shining. The fat leaf buds were bursting, the tender green iridescent in the bright morning sun.

Luke and Louis were standing by the car, smiling. They drove us home. We walked up the stairs into our apartment. The door closed and we flew into each other's arms. We were together again.

180

CHAPTER 10

On Thursday we saw Dr. Abbot. "What plans have you made to go home?"

"None. I had to cancel all my original bookings. I am waiting for you to tell us when we may leave."

"You may leave at the end of next week."

"On Thursday?" I asked hopefully.

"Yes."

Now the days flew past. There was laughter and gaiety. We cooked and ate our meals together. Michèle and Louis drove us to Minneapolis and on the way took Luke and Nicky to a fun fair. We all dined with Peter and Sheila Joubert, and they came and dined with us.

Even the atmosphere at the Clinic was different. The physicians were now relaxed and cheerful, sharing in our happiness.

Our Great Adventure was drawing to a close.

Nicky and I were birds of passage, poised for flight.

I wrote to Dr. Abbot.

"Tomorrow we leave Rochester.

"Before leaving I want to express my deep appreciation for what you have done for us.

"Nicky is on the threshold of a new life: and the beginning of a new life is starting for my husband and me.

"For this I thank you with the deepest gratitude. I thank you too for the tenderness and the kindness you showed Nicky.

"He joins me in sending you our kindest regards."

Dr. Berange I also thanked for his gentleness, and added:

"And I thank you too, for the teasing. Nicky and I will always remember you with great affection."

For those two men to whom we owed so much, I had developed a deep and warm regard.

Five weeks later, when I was dining with the family at Greystones and Sue was also with us, I tried to explain.

I said to Bill:

"I think I fell a little bit in love with both of them."

A loud snort from Bill.

SUE: "Look at Dad's face!"

ME: "Well, I did."

SUE: "You couldn't love them. You couldn't be in love with them. Really, Mom!"

ME: "All I can say is, that when two men are responsible for your son being reborn, and treat him with such kindness and gentleness, you love them. Do you think I could say in my book—I fell a little bit in love with both of them?"

Loud family chorus (Bill's voice loudest of all): "No!!"

SUE: "Why don't you say—I felt something for them akin to love."

ME: (resigned) "Very well."

I felt something for them akin to love.

For my last meeting with them, I put on my most elegant

suit, my pearls and my diamond brooch. I was under no illusions that it would make any impression on Dr. Abbot, but I had greater hopes of Dr. Berange.

Sure enough, when he saw me, he tilted an expressive Gallic eyebrow and made an appreciative sound.

I hoped that Dirk would one day show the same gallantry towards a woman old enough to be his mother.

He examined Nicky for the last time.

"He is excellent. I teenk one day he will be very tall."

When he left we shook hands.

"Good-by, Dr. Berange. Thank you for the wonderful way you looked after Nicky, and for everything you did for him."

"You will write at Christmas? You will let us know how he is getting on?"

"Of course."

Considerably later Dr. Abbot entered. His manner, as always, was precise and to the point.

"Nicky must continue to take Digitalis for three months. He must remain on the first diet for six weeks."

I groaned inwardly.

"As from when?" I asked hopefully.

"As from now!" he said, with a close approach to a grin. "He must then remain on the second diet for a month. He must be kept very quiet for the next three months and must not go to school. How do your terms work?"

"It will work very well. There are another six weeks of this term left and then the long June holidays come. He won't miss more than a term and a half of school altogether."

"Good. In three months we would like to have a report on him."

He paused.

"Keep him very quiet, try not to let him do too much. The next three months are very important. He is going to be fine."

He smiled and held his hand out to Nicky.

"Good-by, Nicky."

183

I rose and we shook hands.

"Good-by, Dr. Abbot—and thank you." I tried to put all that I felt into those two inadequate words.

His smile was charming.

"You're welcome," he said.

And he was gone.